SCOTTISH COUNTRY

Scottish Country

CHARLES MACLEAN

CHRISTOPHER SIMON SYKES

With over 400 illustrations in colour

THAMES AND HUDSON

ALSO BY CHARLES MACLEAN

ISLAND ON THE EDGE OF THE WORLD
THE WOLF CHILDREN
THE WATCHER

ALSO BY CHRISTOPHER SIMON SYKES

ENGLISH COUNTRY (with Caroline Seebohm)
PRIVATE LANDSCAPES (with Caroline Seebohm)

PHOTO CREDITS page 25 (bottom left): © Mark Fiennes; pages 90, 92
(left); 94, 95 (top): Glasgow Museums: Art Gallery and Museum,
Kelvingrove; pages 95 (bottom), 169 (center): © Windsor Castle, Royal
Library. Her Majesty Queen Elizabeth II; page 166 (bottom center): Royal
Museum of Scotland.

In memory of Irene Stirling

*For Margaret Augusta and
Katharine Alexandra*
C. M.

For Joseph and Lily
C. S. S.

THE AUTHORS WOULD LIKE TO THANK HER MAJESTY QUEEN ELIZABETH THE QUEEN MOTHER FOR GIVING THEM HER GRACIOUS PERMISSION TO PHOTOGRAPH BIRKHALL. THEY ARE GRATEFUL TO ALL THE OWNERS OF THE HOUSES AND GARDENS THAT APPEAR IN THIS BOOK FOR THEIR GENEROUS COOPERATION, HELPFUL ADVICE, AND UNFAILING HOSPITALITY.

THE AUTHORS WOULD ALSO LIKE TO PAY A SPECIAL TRIBUTE TO GAEL TOWEY AND BARBARA PECK, WHO WORKED SO HARD ON THE BEAUTIFUL DESIGN OF THE BOOK, A TASK GAEL TOOK ON IN SPITE OF MANY OTHER COMMITMENTS (INCLUDING A NEW BABY!), AND TO CAROL SOUTHERN AND ELIZA SCOTT, WHO STRUGGLED BRAVELY AND PATIENTLY TO CARRY OUT THE VISION OF TWO ELUSIVE PEOPLE ON THE OTHER SIDE OF THE OCEAN.

THE AUTHORS ALSO WISH TO ACKNOWLEDGE *HG* AS THE ORIGINAL PUBLISHERS OF SOME OF THE MATERIAL USED IN THE CHAPTERS ON GARDENS, STRACHUR, AND ARDKINGLAS.

PREVIOUS PAGE, *the Isle of Jura.* LEFT, *the view across to the Paps of Jura from the Isle of Oronsay.* OVERLEAF, *vale of Strathmore looking north to the Highlands.*

CONTENTS

Although we lived in England until I was eleven, I was brought up to think of Scotland as my real home and of my family as an unfortunate band of exiles. Every summer we made a holiday pilgrimage to the Highlands, cheering in triumph as we crossed the border on our way north and enjoying, from that moment on, a month of freedom from the polite restraints of English county life. We stayed, billeted on my Fraser cousins, in the privileged orbit of Beaufort Castle, a splendid baronial pile and clan chief's seat on the banks of the river Beauly. It was an idyllic, untrammeled world, especially for us children, who spent all our time outdoors and were taught how to fish and shoot in the justified context of learning to live off the land. Naturally it reinforced my impression of Scotland as a near-fabulous country—the kind of place a sensible person would choose never to leave.

The price we happily paid for being allowed to run wild over my uncle's far-flung estates was long hours of indentured labor. One of my earliest Beaufort memories is of joining a line of barefoot, kilted cousins and being set to work every morning in the fields below the castle clearing the land of stones and ragwort—the yel-low-flowered, tenacious weed better known in the Highlands as "Stinkin' Willy." Named after the Duke of Cumberland, who commanded the Hanoverian forces that butchered the Highland clans at the Battle of Culloden, it gave our unpleasant, lost cause of a task a patriotic savor: We were rewarded according to who could root out the greatest number of these ideologically unacceptable invaders.

By the time my father, a peripatetic clan chieftain, returned to settle in the Highlands, I had acquired a somewhat wider experience of the Scottish scene. After spending a few winters in Argyll, my exile's romantic *amor patriae* was tempered by the realities of leading a remote existence in an unforgiving climate. It was not until I came back to live permanently in Scotland with my own family, after years of being schooled and working in the south and abroad, that I really began to get to know my own country. As I watched my children grow up here, taking for granted the commonplace pleasures and trials of Highland life, I began to share their unquestioning sense of belonging.

Traveling the length and breadth of the Scottish countryside in gathering material for this book, I have had my eyes opened again by working with Christopher Sykes, whose visual acumen and (in some ways) more objective viewpoint saved us on a few occasions from presenting the familiar heather-and-haggis image of "Bonnie Scotland." Hoping to dispel the popular notion of the Scottish country house as a grim, rain-lashed fortress with thickets of antlers on the clammy stone walls and nothing but a few tartan rugs to keep out the chill of centuries, our aim has been to reveal, through Scotland's less well-known houses—from croft to castle,

farm-house to Georgian mansion, tower house to Victorian shooting lodge—and through its gardens and landscapes, an identifiably Scottish style.

There is always a danger (especially when a *non*-Scot is involved) of getting carried away by the idea of Scottishness. Few countries of Scotland's size, it must be said, have contributed more to the world. Think only of the Adam brothers, Charles Rennie Mackintosh, Allan Ramsay, Robert Burns, Hume, Sir Walter Scott, Carlyle, Adam Smith, Robert Louis Stevenson; of the steam engine, television, whisky, golf. . . . The patents and resources of Scottish identity are legion. Style, on the other hand, is a more elusive quality. But the private, mostly unexampled, often eccentric portrait that emerges from Christopher's sympathetic photographs comes close to capturing the true spirit of Scottish country life.

The houses in their landscapes tell a small part of Scotland's story, tracing the fitful evolution of Scottish architecture and domestic traditions. Chosen for their intrinsic appeal rather than any representative qualities, they illustrate nonetheless a simple premise: that the multiform beauty of the land shaped the ways in which Scots, throughout their troubled history, have lived in harmony with an environment that offered them greater hardship than reward, yet always inspired fierce loyalty and a passionate love of country.

LEFT, *a tributary burn cascades down the steep slopes of An Teallach, which rises 3,500 feet above the Dundonnell river.*

On reaching the top of Foinaven, an ancient craggily distinguished hill in the far north of Scotland, I looked down onto a vast treeless mosaic of land and water, which, fading at its edges into coastal haze, bore no signs of man's present or past influence. As far as I could see in any direction, even out toward Cape Wrath and the Pentland Firth, the wilderness, silent except for the wind and occasional bird's cry, stretched away irredeemably bleak and inhospitable. Here, it seemed, in its desolate beauty was the quintessential Highland country, the reassuring image of unlimited space and pristine nature that is readily identified with Scotland and, lately, has come to be valued as the last great tract of wild, unspoiled country in Europe.

Indeed, rugged hill ground accounts for three-quarters of the Scottish landscape; yet the magnificent Highland scenery we emote over, merchandise to tourists, and jealously protect is in fact a devastated area, a man-made wilderness of no less discreditable origin than America's Dust Bowl. Most of Scotland was once covered by lush forest, the great Caledonian pinewood (straggly remnants of which can still be seen from Rannoch Moor to Speyside) that over the millennia man has destroyed. Baring the hills of trees and shelter, he overgrazed the pasture that succeeded the forest, and by long misuse of the land reduced it to its present barren state. The land (due to accidents of geology and eternal bad weather) was inherently poor, but it once supported considerable human populations where now there are none. In many parts of the Highlands, which rate today as wilderness, old cultivation ridges and the faint outline of enclosures bear witness to abandoned settlements, some lost by attrition over the centuries, others cleared after the break-up of the clan system to make room for more profitable populations of sheep and deer. Yet at the same time that the massive introduction of sheep was despoiling the limited and fragile resources of the Highlands, to the south lairds and landowners inspired by the agricultural revolution began to replant trees and transform the Lowland countryside into a settled pastoral landscape.

Two hundred and fifty years ago, most people's idea of Scotland was confined to a not very flattering view of the Lowlands; the Highlands were thought of (if thought of at all) as an alien waste inhabited by savage tribes more remote from the salons of London *and* Edinburgh than the wilds of Afghanistan. Even today, a traveler crossing the border from England—though he no longer takes his life in his hands, as he would have in the eighteenth century—is immediately

A high, desolate loch among the ancient rocks of Foinaven in the far north of Scotland, RIGHT.

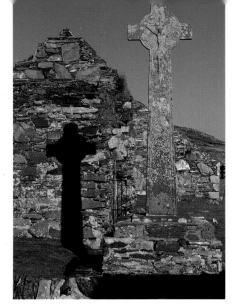

aware of entering a foreign country. One might almost say a foreign continent for, going back some 500 million years, Scotland and England were separated by an ocean. Where I stood last year among the ancient rocks of Foinaven, I would once have been standing in North America. England then was a part of Europe. The geological cataclysms that first brought the two countries together in violent union have as much to answer for as the later tectonic upheavals and shrouds of ice that shaped the dramatic Scottish countryside, making it a land of extraordinary physical contrasts and, in as much as geography shapes destiny, human contradictions.

The geographical divides that separate the Highlands and Islands, Lowland and Border regions have their equivalents in history, customs, and language (to the Gaelic-speaking Highlander, the Lallan dialects spoken in the Borders sound as foreign as Swahili). Such rich diversity may be appealing but often makes it difficult to talk about Scotland as one country. Nonetheless, from its earliest beginnings, the history of all Scotland has imprinted itself in stone upon the landscape. Neolithic stone circles, brochs and duns (fortified stone towers) built by Iron Age Celts, Pictish carvings, the monkish cells and Celtic crosses of early Christian missionaries, the residue of Roman and Norse attempts at colonization, still feature sturdily in the Scottish countryside, if only because

later interference from people and agriculture in remote areas has been minimal. On the west coast, particularly in the Hebridean islands, the stones lend a feeling of ancient meaning to the land that can easily be confused, given the natural religiousness of the people, with a mystical legacy. Walking among the ecclesiastical ruins of Oronsay or Iona, where in A.D. 563 St. Columba founded the monastery that made this tiny island the center of Christian Europe, it's tempting to imagine that years of spiritual brightness have left a numinous impression.

The forging of a national identity, which occupied the Scots over the dark and epically bloody centuries leading up to the early Middle Ages, culminated in the struggle for independence led by King Robert the Bruce. The decisive defeat he inflicted on the English army at the Battle of Bannockburn in 1314 gave birth to the idea of a Scottish nation. Despite diverse interests constantly threatening its fragile unity, and despite the relinquishment of sovereignty in 1707, the dream of nationhood has never let go its hold on

Another splendid view of Foinaven, ABOVE LEFT. ABOVE CENTER, *the standing stones at Callanish on Lewis in the Outer Hebrides rival Stonehenge in their mystery and beauty.* ABOVE RIGHT, *a Celtic cross on the island of Oronsay. The relief of the Crucifixion was added later and is dated 1510.*

the Scottish consciousness. No less pertinent to an understanding of what it means to be Scottish is the Celtic legacy of the clan system, which was the major form of social organization for more than a thousand years and still survives today, if chiefly in sentimental rituals and never-quite-forgotten rivalries. There are Macdonalds who to this day will not shake hands with a Campbell, looking back with unexorcised memories to the Massacre of Glencoe. In February 1692, a party of Campbell troops billeted on the Macdonalds of Glencoe rose in the night and, acting on government orders, did their best to slaughter their hosts, men, women, and children. The incident achieved lasting notoriety less as an atrocity—too many surpassed it for bloody rapaciousness and treachery—than as a breech of the Highland laws of hospitality. Still a significant aspect of Highland life, as anyone who has attended a *ceilidh* (an informal gathering enlivened by music, dancing, and whisky at which strangers are always welcome) can testify, the gift of hospitality may be typical of remote and lonely mountain districts where neighbors are far and few, but in Scotland it has its origins in the Highlander's staunch code of morality and honor and in the very nature of clannish pride.

Clan, or *clann* in Gaelic, means children. In the context of an extended tribal family, the chief of a clan was literally father of his people. He was of the same blood as his clansmen; he commanded their absolute loyalty, wielding the power of life and death over all who bore his name; and he shared with them the land, cattle, and endless disputes from which the clan drew its living and identity. The clan system was not restricted to the Highlands; there were just as many powerful Lowland and Border families, but their organization was more feudal than patriarchal, effectively separating the Highlands and Lowlands into two different and opposing worlds. Whereas under feudalism all land belonged to the crown, which had final authority over the Lowland chiefs, among the Highland clans the land was held communally and administered as an independent principality by the chief, to whom the clansmen willingly gave the allegiance of kin, not of vassal subjects.

In the Highlands, a dangerous place of shifting alliances and simmering conflicts, kinship was (and to a certain extent still is) of paramount importance. If there was such a thing

ABOVE LEFT, *the entrance hall of The Drum, a c. 1730 Palladian house outside Edinburgh built by William Adam, boasts opulent plasterwork probably by Dutch craftsmen.* ABOVE RIGHT, *the remains of the broch at Dun Carloway on the island of Lewis. A circular defensive tower, it was built around the beginning of the Christian era.*

as a clan philosophy, no one put it more clearly than my ancestor, Simon, eleventh Lord Lovat, a wily old turncoat admired in Gaeldom as a great clan chief, who said: "There is nothing I place in balance with my kindred." Or they, one might add, with him. For every Highlander, able to trace his descent from the same name-fathers of the great historic clans—from Somerled Lord of the Isles, from Gillean of the Battleaxe, from Gregor of the Golden Bridles, and others— shared with his chief a pride of race that made him, regardless of material wealth or status, a genealogist and a gentleman, who knew that only the ties of blood could "withstand the rocks."

But by the beginning of the eighteenth century, the Highlanders' contempt of government and dependence on plunder as their economic mainstay had become a faltering anachronism. The clan system, fragmented by the ill-fated Jacobite rebellions, did not survive the defeat of Bonnie Prince Charlie at Culloden in 1746. After the battle, the clans loyal to the Stewart cause were punished with spectacular brutality by the Duke of Cumberland, eagerly assisted by both English and Lowland Scottish government troops. Lands were forfeited, the chiefs stripped of their powers, the clans disarmed, and Highland dress proscribed—even the bagpipes were banned as "an instrument of war"—in a determined effort finally to eradicate the Highland menace.

In the century that followed, the story of the Highlands makes dismal reading. The process of destruction started by Cumberland's troops was exacerbated by an unprecedented population explosion and economic hardship that led, among other failed solutions, to wholesale evictions and forced emigration. Many of the clan chiefs and lairds (though by no means all) played a discreditable part in the Highland Clearances. Reduced by the government in London to mere landlords, they abandoned their former sense of responsibility

LEFT, *a charming farmhouse in Skye.*

for their clansmen and assumed a proprietor's right to turn their lands into sheep farms and sporting estates in the hope of making them pay. Others, often with equally disastrous results, tried to preserve the old dependencies. But the spirit of the clans was broken, the old way of life gone forever. The tragic and still emotive aspect of the Clearances was that the clansman's passionate attachment to his native territory defined his universe; to be removed by his own kin from the land that for centuries their common ancestors had fought and died for seemed an incomprehensible betrayal. The lament of the dispossessed, poignantly expressed in the anonymous song of a nineteenth-century exile to Canada, has lost none of its power to stir Scottish hearts:

From the lone shieling of the misty island
Mountains divide us, and the waste of seas;
Yet still the blood is strong, the heart is Highland
And we in dreams behold the Hebrides.

For those Highlanders who stayed behind, the alternative to enlisting in the newly formed Highland Regiments or drifting into overcrowded cities was to eke out a precarious existence as crofters on land so marginal it was considered unfit even for sheep. These crofts (from the Gaelic *croit*), small pieces of arable land which the crofter rented on a yearly basis (until the 1886 Crofting Act gave him security of tenure), were supplemented by access to common grazing land shared within the crofting township or community. An ecologically sound form of land use suited to the Highlands and Islands, crofting had then as now the important social effect of keeping parts of the country populated that would otherwise have become wilderness. As a way of life, though it may have been arduous and limiting, crofting perpetuated the windowless "black house," with its thick rubble walls and turf roof, the most basic and characteristic form of rural Scottish architecture; it also preserved something of the old fiercely independent yet communal character of the High-

lands that as much as its romantic castles or picturesque scenery explains Scotland's universal allure.

It is surely revealing that no sooner had Britain rid itself of the troublesome clans than a movement began to salvage and honor their memory. Stirred up by the historical novels of Sir Walter Scott and perpetuated by Queen Victoria's famous weakness for the Highlands, the craze for clan tartans, for ruins and dramatic landscapes, for salmon-fishing and stalking, for all things Scottish has never really lost momentum or touched the ground since. The millions of tourists who flock to Scotland every year in search of unspoiled wilderness, lost ancestors, or Japanese-owned whisky distilleries, may discover little evidence of "Clan Scotland" behind the tartan veil other than the tawdry spectacle of a Highland Games. Yet some benefits of the clan system have survived, finding vestigial expression in the natural pride and warmth of a people for whom the bonds of kinship once produced vertical as opposed to horizontal social distinctions that cut across the Anglo-Saxon preoccupation with class. In the recruitment of both Highland and Lowland regiments. In the fact that there are no laws of trespass in Scotland, a watered-down legacy of the clan ownership of land. Or, as the character of the houses (large and small) featured in this book reveals, in an affectionate but not stifling regard for family history and for the legends and traditions of the Scottish countryside.

The pages that follow can give little more than an impressionistic view of Scotland's domestic architecture, just as the houses themselves allow only local glimpses into the bewildering complexities of Scottish history or the enigmatic Scottish character. Scotland's great country houses and castles—Falkland, Drumlanrig, Glamis, Castle Fraser, Inveraray, Hopetoun, Cawdor, Culzean, and Balmoral, to name a few—are not represented here, though as the source of the main trends and themes of Scottish architecture their presence makes itself felt. Aside from shunning the over-familiar, there was little method to our selection of houses beyond personal preference. If no manse (in the Scot's sense of a Presbyterian minister's dwelling) has been included, despite its interest as an architectural type and the enormous influence of the Kirk on Scottish country life, it is only because we never found one we liked. An obvious omission, for which we make no apology, is the vast neobaronial "castle" that sprang up in the late nineteenth century, often as an adornment to the great Victorian sporting estates, and that created a false, absurdly pompous stereotype of Scottish style.

One advantage of looking at lesser buildings is that not being so susceptible to foreign influences and fashions they preserved the vernacular traditions longer. What is remarkable about the houses in this book is that (with one modern exception) they could not be anything else but Scottish. Their distinctiveness from their English equivalents can be explained by Scotland's stubborn determination to retain a separate identity from its larger and more powerful neighbor. Indeed, until the eighteenth century, there was only limited contact between the two countries, Scotland's main trading partners being Holland, Scandinavia, and the Baltic seaboard, while its natural political and cultural ally was France. The "Auld Alliance," as it came to be known, is often held responsible for a French accent in Scottish architecture, typically, the more indulgent flourishes of the Jacobean tower houses. If anything, the Scots resisted Gallic as firmly as they did Anglo-Saxon styles, though in other ways they welcomed France's civilizing influence, which had them drinking the finest clarets while the English were still quaffing mead.

The late eighteenth century saw a greater economic prosperity in Scotland due in part to the 1707 Act of Union (between England and Scotland) and to the flowering of the Scottish Enlightenment, which brought about social changes (promoted by a Government edict forcing clan chiefs and lairds to educate their eldest sons in the south) that inevitably closed the gap between Scottish and English tastes in archi-

tecture. Ironically, while Scotland produced some of the Georgian age's most popular architects, including James Gibbs, Sir William Chambers, Colin Campbell, and Charles Cameron, they mostly lived and worked abroad. The Scots were never quite rich enough, nor perhaps sufficiently pleased with themselves, to build in the grand manner. Only William Adam and his more famous sons John, Robert, and James, Scotland's preeminent architectural family, did much work in their own country, lending their name to a classical style that has never been surpassed as the gentlemanly ideal of country living.

What seems most characteristic about Scotland's architecture is not its simple, rebarbative masculinity—the reliance for aesthetic effect on massive form, robust proportions, and restrained use of ornament—but the impression old Scottish houses give of having literally grown out of the countryside. The emphasis on siting buildings defensively or on finding a spot sheltered from the wind and rain, as well as the use of sympathetic local materials, produced the pleasing effect of houses sensibly adapted to a demanding human and physical environment. The wild grandeur of the landscape, its beauties as well as its inhospitable barrenness, has long kept the Scots countryman in a close, respectful relationship with nature. Whether it can continue to do so in an age of oil exploration, commercial forestry, mass tourism, fish farms, and acid rain no longer seems certain. The last wilderness in Europe, like last wildernesses everywhere, is threatened. But Scotland remains one of the few countries where there still exists a recognizable harmony between architecture and countryside. The contrast of elegance and ruggedness that enhances most aspects of our cultural inheritance reflects above all a pride in adversity, which is the genius of Scottish history and the source of Scotland's highly individual indigenous style.

RIGHT, *Castle Stalker, built in the early-sixteenth century, rises proudly from its own small island in Loch Linnhe.*

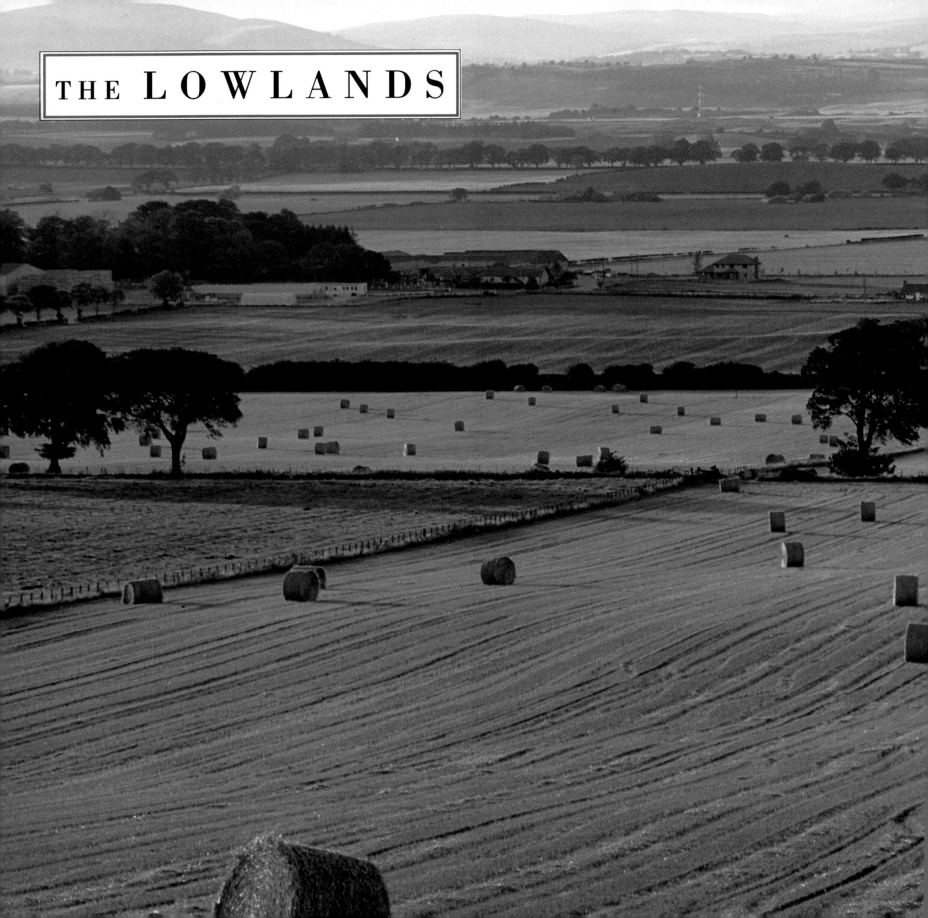

THE LOWLANDS

SHA

Under the wintry brow of Arnton Fell, the farmhouse at Shaws, RIGHT. Detail of an angel from nearby Hermitage Castle, LEFT.

WS FARM

WHEN SIR WALTER SCOTT WAS COLLECT-
ing material for his *Minstrelsy of the Scottish Border,* making his annual "raids" into Liddesdale,
he would wander over its bleak moors and wild-
flower-rich lees, exploring every ruined tower
and tracking down any local who could still sing
the ballads of the mosstroopers, the old Border
raiders, whose exploits reverberate across the
centuries in what many consider the finest body
of folk poetry ever recorded. On these romantic
forays into the "Debatable Land," Scott stayed at
a friend's house a mile from where Shaws Farm
now stands overlooking—in winter, at least,
when the trees are bare—the impressive ruin of
Hermitage Castle. The "Strength of Liddesdale," as it was known, built by the English, captured and rebuilt by the Scottish Earls of
Douglas, Hermitage characterized the violent,
treachery-darkened years of conflict on the Border throughout the Middle Ages. Even as late as
the 1790s, Liddesdale was still wild and inacces-
sible enough for Walter Scott's horse-drawn car-
riage to cause a sensation in the villages as the
poet passed through, notebook in hand.

In the early part of the nineteenth century,
the Dukes of Buccleuch, whose estates incorpo-
rated most of Liddesdale, made a determined
effort to deliver their territory from the primi-
tivism of its haunted past. Their Graces went on
an improvements splurge, sparing no expense
in raising a crop of fine stone farmhouses and
steadings, even whole villages, for their tenants.
Shaws Farm, which was built in 1823—though

*The red drawing room at
Shaws,* ABOVE.

the well-worn stone stair leading to the cellar
suggests that there may have been an earlier
house on the site—is a typically tall and handsome example of Buccleuch largesse. Plain, austere, yet ingenuously grand for a farmhouse, it
lies anchored in the windswept landscape under
the cambered brow of Arnton Fell. Built of local
sandstone, once blackened with pitch to keep
out the wet, now rendered less severe by out-
breaks of ivy and climbing roses, Shaws still
seems in its stark foursquareness a domestic
echo of Hermitage Castle.

The house and farm were sold by the Buc-

cleuch estates in 1947, and after a period of drift and decline were taken on by the present owner, who grew up on an estate near Peebles and knew what he was letting himself and his family in for. Although turning Shaws into a going concern has meant years of hard work, there have been no regrets. In dilapidated condition, the house and its original steading, which were built to the same high standard—even the dog kennels are made of dressed stone—were in need of restoration. The traditional drystane walls that fence in the owner's sheep and cattle were all in danger of collapsing and had to be

A rag-rug sheep warms itself over the kitchen Aga, ABOVE LEFT, *which provides a constant source of heat that is sometimes used for drying clothes as well as for cooking.* ABOVE RIGHT, *butterflies and berries over a vase of dried flowers.*

rebuilt, as did the pedestrian suspension bridge over Hermitage Water, the trout-filled burn that flows through the 1,500-acre farm. The bridge may or may not have been the work of Thomas Telford, the great Scottish engineer and bridge builder, who came from nearby Langholm, but is an interesting example of the suspension principle, widely believed north of the Border to be a local invention.

Life at Shaws generally conforms to the pattern of the farming year. According to season, the larder bulges with home-produced fruit and vegetables, eggs and butter, meat and game. A

throwback to the traditional way of life that so many farmers have abandoned, the economy of the house seems a model of self-sufficiency. Again reverting to a vanished tradition, the interior decorations at Shaws are mostly drawn from nature. Every wall in the house is covered with pictures of flowers, ranging from the efforts of local artists to Elizabeth Blackadders (bought before she became one of Scotland's most acclaimed painters) to Thornton's "Temple of Flora." The owner's wife, who is an accomplished artist, claims she does not consciously collect flower paintings. Inspired by

The artist in her studio, ABOVE RIGHT, overlooking the garden where she grows the kinds of flowers that she likes to paint. The ideas for her rag rugs also come from the natural world around her. THIS PAGE and OPPOSITE, a selection of her watercolors and rag rugs. The landscapes were inspired by her travels through Scotland and have the immediacy of journal entries.

Blackadder's early drawings, she turned her own botanical knowledge and pleasure in flowers to artistic account and began to fill the house with the work of other flower painters as well as her own.

When she took it over, the walled garden at Shaws was waist-high in nettles and brambles and had to be ploughed up and started again from scratch. Now fruit, flowers, and vegetables grow there in astonishing plenty, though coming across unusual or eccentric plants—the striped rose Souvenir de Ferdinand Pichard, Martagon lilies, even the emblematic Scotch this-

tle—reminds one that the garden was designed by an artist. "I paint flowers, so I very largely grow what I want to paint," she explains. From the window of her studio, converted from a shed in the old steading, she can see into the heart of the garden and, all summer long, raid the flower beds for whatever buds, blossoms, or greenery she needs. In winter, she transfers her studio to the warmth of the farm kitchen; and her talent to the making of rag rugs out of hessian sacks and old clothes.

A traditional Borders craft, rag rugs were found in every farm in the Lowlands until

OVERLEAF: *The entrance hall,* TOP LEFT, *and the tack room,* BOTTOM LEFT, *reveal the wide range of country pursuits that are part of life at Shaws. The larder,* TOP CENTER, *fills with homegrown food according to season. Baskets for picnics, gardening, and fruit-picking hang under traditional farmhouse cupboards. The farmyard sounds of Cheviot sheep,* RIGHT, *and chickens can be heard from the nearby steading,* BOTTOM CENTER.

they began to disappear soon after World War II, tainted by their association with "making do" or poverty. As for technique, Shaws' resident artist follows the old ways, but in choice of design and subject matter, she has spread her wings. "I still get my ideas by looking out of the window, the flowers in the garden, animals in the field. I think it would be a mistake to do Princess Anne on her horse, or Sir Walter Scott striding over Liddesdale. . . ." By a twist of history, rag rugs continue to be made in North America, the last place on earth, as it happens, where the Border ballads are still sung.

AUC

LEFT *and* RIGHT, *elegant steps lead up to the Renaissance doorway of Auchindinny House in Midlothian, one of the last and most attractive houses designed by Scotland's first architect, Sir William Bruce. Apart from the dormer windows, the house has been little altered since it was built in 1707.*

HINDINNY

IF THE MISSING PLANS OF AUCHINDINNY House in Midlothian ever come to light, they will no doubt show that it was raised over the foundations of a much earlier tower or fortified manor house. The vaulted ceilings and massive walls (in places eight feet thick) of the moated basement are clearly superfluous to the defensive needs of this small, charmingly domestic Queen Anne country house. But, as medieval remnants, they would have appealed to Auchindinny's architect, Sir William Bruce, who, whenever possible, built onto or over ancient structures as a way of establishing a sense of continuity. The penultimate, and perhaps most attractive, house that Bruce designed, Auchin-

The symbol of the sun inside the pediment over the front door, ABOVE, *was to let the local fire brigade know that the house was insured.* TOP, *an outdoor bench and chairs, dappled with sunlight.*

dinny was completed in 1707, the year of the Act of Union with England, when the Scots gave up their independence—not without confusion, resentment, or protest—for the promise of greater prosperity.

In some ways, while looking forward to a more graceful age, Auchindinny reflects Bruce's loyalties to his country's past. Though laid out in the classical manner with twin pavilions linked to the main house by curved screen walls (a miniature version of his own house at Kinross), Auchindinny harks back to the vernacular style of the previous century. The extreme plainness of the house, its severe geometry softened by modesty of scale, the practical bell-cast roof designed

30

to stay on in a gale, the simple elegance of the steps leading up to the pedimented front door (the single concession to ornament), give the impression of native confidence, an ability to combine the sensible and volatile, which has always been part of both the Scottish character and Scotland's building tradition.

Why a famous architect, who had worked on the great palaces of Holyrood and Hopetoun, should have agreed to take on so insignificant a commission is something of a mystery. Built for John Inglis of Langbyres, a lawyer with a moderately successful practice in Edinburgh, barely ten miles distant, Auchindinny has remained in the Inglis family ever since. The house is now lived in by Inglis's descendant (also an Edinburgh lawyer), who makes the case that Bruce, having fallen on hard times, may have owed his ancestor money—"but not very much money, which is why he built him such a small house." Until 1930, Auchindinny was only used as a summer place by the Inglises, whose main residence was in Edinburgh. Now that the city falls within easy commuting reach, it has become very much the family home, the present occupants' eldest daughter being the first Inglis to have been born in the house.

Apart from some late Georgian dormer windows and a bathroom wing added to the back in 1920—the first internal plumbing the house enjoyed—there have been few alterations to Bruce's original design. The interior, with its central stone staircase and small but well-proportioned rooms paneled in oak and Memel pine, has survived more or less intact. Some of the windows in the dining room are original and still have the sturdy astragals and hand-flung glass panes that are as strongly evocative of period as old photographs. The fact that the house was let out of the family for most of the nineteenth century may well have preserved Auchindinny—as was the case, strangely enough, at Kinross—from Victorian "improvements."

One of Auchindinny's more illustrious tenants was Henry Mackenzie, a close friend of Sir Walter Scott and author of *The Man of Feeling*, an important text of the Scottish Enlightenment. Scott brought his young bride to tea at Auchindinny, and it seems likely that other luminaries from the "Athens of the North," as Edinburgh was known in its golden age, would have found their way there. Mackenzie, whose portrait hangs in the dining room, rented Auchindinny between 1795 and 1807 and refers to Bruce's design of the house in his writings, mentioning the odd but apposite fact that the chimneys never smoked. As is usual in a Bruce building, the chimneys sit in the middle of the roof rather than at the gable ends, which, the present occupants concur, prevents them smoking and helps to keep the house warm and dry. After nearly three hundred years of Scottish weather, that is no inconsiderable recommendation.

The stone stairs, ABOVE, have molded risers identical to the ones on the stairs at the Palace of Holyroodhouse, where Bruce also worked. The flagstoned entrance hall, RIGHT, accommodates family clutter and firewood.

THERE IS AN IRRATIONAL BELIEF IN Scotland that it's unlucky to pull down a doocot (dovecote). It may have originated with a decree passed by James VI, a profoundly superstitious man, making it illegal to destroy doocots. But somewhere between lingering respect for the king's will and a Celtic dread of disturbing the past lies the reason for so many of these picturesque monuments having survived. Living larders where pigeons were kept and fattened for meat, doocots, or pigeon houses, now number about seven hundred in Scotland. The earliest date from the fifteenth century and were usually attached to castles, harking back to a law that allowed only certain powerful lairds to build them and only with royal approval. Although many are still inhabited, they are of more interest today as architectural curiosities than as a safeguard against hunger. In the Highlands, most surviving doocots are found on great estates, reflecting their former importance as status symbols. But essentially doocots were functional farm buildings. The pigeons, or doos, were bred and raised both for their meat, particularly welcome in the winter months after the cattle and sheep had been slaughtered, and for their dung, which provided valuable manure for the fields. When turnips were introduced from the Netherlands in the seventeenth century and it became possible to feed stock through the winter, the English gave up building dovecotes. But agriculture advanced more slowly north of the

DOOCOTS

Formerly a status symbol, the Scottish doocot gave rise to some interesting architectural forms. Boath Doocot, OPPOSITE, *which stands at the edge of a modern housing estate, has a single masonry stringcourse to prevent rats from climbing up into the nesting boxes.*

border, and Scots went on constructing or occasionally converting old towers into doocots until well into the nineteenth century. The harm done to crops by locust-like flocks of pigeons gave rise to a body of Scottish law centered on the question of who should be allowed to have doocots. After 1617, they were confined by law to larger properties; no one could build a doocot unless they owned the land for two miles around the proposed site, thus, in theory, confining the damage the birds caused to the owner's own crops. The birds, however, did not always respect the two-mile limit, nor did the next-door laird or farmer meekly put up with their depredations. Further laws were passed to protect the doocot owner from his irate neighbors. The penalties for breaking into a doocot with a view to stealing or injuring the doos were severe and, at one time, included death. Traveling around Scotland, you come across doocots in the least expected places: in the middle of gardens, open fields, beside motorways, on housing estates. "Spot the doocot" can become an absorbing pastime: I know of one Gothic-looking example just outside Inverness that has been converted into a wonderfully eccentric cottage. Because of the prestige attached to doocots, they offered a rare chance for displaying architectural inventiveness. Doocots were built in all shapes and sizes: round, square, octagonal; styled like towers, lecterns, beehives; decorated with pinnacles, finials, and crow-stepped gables.

Some examples of different doocots. ABOVE, the aptly named *Phantassie Doocot in East Linton, a massive structure with walls four-feet thick at the base and nesting places for five hundred birds. Its sloping horseshoe-shaped roof gives the doos the benefit of southern exposure. Phantassie has been recolonized by wild pigeon, but from a distance it looks as if it landed from Mars.* FAR LEFT, *a Gothic farmyard doocot. A doocot at the bottom of the garden at Crathes Castle,* LEFT. *The doocot at Glamis,* RIGHT, *looks like a lectern made of Lego blocks.*

At the West End of the Lake
(Lochleven) . . . stands the
most beautiful and regular
piece of Architecture (for a
private Gentleman's Seat)
in all Scotland, perhaps in
all Great Britain. The
House is a picture, 'tis all
Beauty, the Stone is white
and fine, the Order regular,
the Contrivance elegant, the
Workmanship exquisite.
            Daniel Defoe, 1722

The east façade of Kinross,
RIGHT, *from the shores of
Loch Leven, showing the
beautiful proportions of the
house. The view from the
porch lines up the formal
garden with the Fish Gate
and the old castle on its
island in the loch.*

KINROSS

The stables and coachhouses, ABOVE, were altered by Sir Basil Montgomery after 1902. Their ogee roofs echo the pavilion, FAR LEFT, attached to the front of the main house by a curved wall. The gardens were re-created by Sir Basil, who made places to sit and enjoy the view and introduced statuary, including Atlas, LEFT, and one of a pair of stone lions, CENTER RIGHT, from Italy. One of four original stone lion heads, FAR RIGHT, with iron rings used to tether horses near the front door. The basket of fish which gave its name to the Fish Gate, the work of Dutch carvers, ABOVE RIGHT, contains examples of the eleven species caught in Loch Leven. The towering doocot, NEAR RIGHT.

At the end of the magnificent salon, or ballroom, ABOVE, hangs a fine portrait by Raeburn, OPPOSITE, of Helen Graham, who inherited the house and married Sir James Montgomery in the nineteenth century. The sitting room, BELOW, reveals the relative compactness of the interior, which gives the house its family atmosphere.

IF HE COULD SEE KINROSS TODAY, THE author of *Robinson Crusoe* would have little cause to revise his judgment. The color of the stone may have deepened, but the house itself has remained almost exactly as Sir William Bruce, Scotland's first, and some say greatest, architect, planned it three hundred years ago. Preserved by its curious history, Kinross has never been structurally altered. A rare example of late-seventeenth-century Scottish architecture, the house Bruce built for himself on a virgin site—his earlier work had been confined to renovation—was an entirely new type of dwelling for Scotland. In a land of rough stone towers and drafty castles, still dominated by an arrow-slit view of the world, Kinross must have seemed extraordinarily alien with its new-fangled sash windows and continental airs and graces.

Bruce has sometimes been called Scotland's Inigo Jones because he imported a European style, laying the ground rules of classicism north of the border. He bought Kinross from the Douglas family in 1675, setting out the policies and gardens before beginning to build four years later. Certainly there is no mistaking the architect's foreign debt: to Serlio for the low attics and division of the façade into rectangles framed by huge Corinthian pilasters; to Palladio for its curved screen walls ending in ogee-roofed pavilions. Bruce's admiration of Le Nôtre, whose work he knew from the château of Vaux-le-Vicomte near Paris, may also have influenced his designs. Yet, from every approach, Kinross

gives a satisfying, unmistakably Scottish sense of mass, a native solidity emphasized by the bold way the architect situated his house and garden in the Scottish landscape.

Although nothing remains of the original parterre—the present garden was reestablished by Sir Basil Montgomery in 1900—the walls and terraces are those laid out by Bruce. He designed them and lined up the axis of the house to focus on a distant prospect of Loch Leven Castle through the "Fish Gate," named after a carving of a bowl of fish representing the eleven species caught in the loch. The formal view, one of the most delightful in Scotland, really begins a quarter of a mile away at the entrance gates. Standing in the middle of the house, the through vista extends from front gates to rear: from the sweeping symmetry of lawns, terraces, and topiary hedges out to open countryside;

The pillared vestibule, ABOVE RIGHT, *Palladian in style, leads into the drawing room,* RIGHT, *which was named the Garden Room by Bruce for its splendid views across the formal gardens to the loch and beyond. A Jacobite recruiting poster,* ABOVE LEFT, *over a fireplace shows Bonnie Prince Charlie wearing tartan.*

from the old town of Kinross down to the romantic ruin of the loch, where in 1568 Mary Queen of Scots spent a year in prison. A Douglas stronghold at the time, Loch Leven Castle, on its own wooded island, was considered a secure fortress, but Mary's jailers underestimated the young queen's negotiable charms, and one of the Douglas sons in "a phantasy of love" helped her to escape.

Bruce couldn't resist establishing links with the past in his buildings, always finding a way to express his love of tradition, his Scottishness. For all its brave new architecture, he made sure that Kinross paid homage in its historical setting to the old Scotland. The second son of a minor Perthshire laird, Bruce owed his patronage and political rise to his support for the exiled Stewarts. After the Restoration, he was appointed Royal Surveyor and Architect in Scotland to

Charles II, for whom he redesigned the Palace of Holyroodhouse in Edinburgh. A gifted amateur with other interests besides architecture—among various public offices he was the local Member of Parliament—Bruce built Kinross, remarkably, in his declining years. When James II came to the throne in 1685, the architect fell from favor and this ambitious, costly enterprise (one theory has it that he could only have intended such a grand house as a royal residence) drained his resources. He never lived at Kinross, but stayed nearby while building was going on and, in 1693, installed his son in his never-quite-completed, but finest, creation.

The interior of the house, spacious, well-proportioned, and richly appointed was as radical a departure from the old Scots Baronial style as the exterior. Gracious reception rooms, connected by tiny corkscrew stairs to pages' quarters below, suggest the growing desire for greater ease and comfort in Scottish life. The magnificent staircase, carved by Dutch craftsmen who were working on the restoration of Holyroodhouse Palace, rises gradually under a fine ornamented ceiling. Bruce ran out of money before he could decorate the Great Salon, a splendid double-height ballroom that runs almost the length of the house. The challenge of completing its ceiling was left to Sir Basil Montgomery, who, taking the plasterwork over the main stairs as a model, finished the salon in the early 1900s.

"He really didn't do a bad job," says Sir David Montgomery, the present owner, who was

The main stair, ABOVE, elaborately carved from oak by the Dutchman Jan Sant Voort. RIGHT, one of the bedrooms at Kinross, which, due to Bruce's declining fortunes, were less sumptuous than the ground-floor rooms.

brought up at Kinross and has lived there with his family since 1972. Although an impractical space, impossible to heat, the ballroom is still used for musical evenings, social functions, and even the occasional ball. At one end, a full-length portrait of Helen Graham by Sir Henry Raeburn reveals, in its depiction of her striking beauty, how Kinross came into Montgomery hands. In 1777, Sir William Bruce's descendants sold the estate to East India merchants called Graham, who lived at Kinross until 1820, when the last male Graham died leaving the house to whichever of his two daughters produced a son first. "The Montgomery of the day got off the mark like a shot," Sir David relates, "and married Helen, who gave birth to a boy six months before her less-pretty sister—which, I might add, is the only reason we're here today."

For the rest of the century, the Montgomerys went on living at their ancestral home, Stobo Castle in Peebleshire, while Kinross, left shuttered up and unoccupied from 1820 to 1900, slept through the Victorian period and thus avoided the fate of "Balmoralization." Kinross was later reclaimed and refurbished by Sir Basil Montgomery, who was perhaps its first owner to appreciate that he had inherited a masterpiece, the summation of what a great architect cherished most in architecture and one of very few Scottish houses that could compete, when it was built, with the sophistication of grand English mansions, or can compare now in its perfection with the great Renaissance châteaux of France.

THE IRONY OF A KILTED HIGHLANDER with targe and claymore slashing his way through a thicket of flowers on an eighteenth-century teapot—or, for that matter, of Bonnie Prince Charlie, deployed between a thistle and a rose, adorning a tartan punch bowl—is that such Jacobite mementos were for the most part produced, soon after the events they commemorated, by English potteries. It was not until the second half of the eighteenth century, when Scotland's economy began to recover from years of stagnation, that pottery production could seriously be considered a Scottish enterprise. Even then, it was the pioneering work of English artisans inveigled into settling in Glasgow and East Lothian, the two centers of pottery manufacturing, that helped develop Scottish craftsmanship and create an industry. **A** wide range of ceramic wares was made in Scotland, from fine porcelain to rough fireclays, but the backbone of the industry was its domestic stoneware. Among various techniques used to decorate the ware (including hand-painting and printing by transfer), sponge-printing, which involved dabbing color onto fired but unglazed ware with a cut sponge, became a Scottish speciality. Cheap, homely, but with a certain ornamental charm, spongeware was produced in great quantities between 1850 and 1925. Although it was widely exported, and can still be found in many a household where "nothing is thrown away," Scottish spongeware has recently been revived by modern craft pot-

POTTERY

OPPOSITE, *stags and hinds decorate the interior of a transferware punch bowl, which was made in Glasgow in the late-nineteenth century by Pollockshaw.*

ters. **S**ome of the smaller Scottish potteries, such as Dunmore in Stirlingshire and the Fife pottery of Robert Heron and Son, makers of Wemyss Ware, aimed at a more sophisticated market and displayed remarkable individuality and inventiveness. Dunmore Ware, renowned for its unconventional shapes and adventurous glazes, enjoyed a wave of popularity at the end of the nineteenth century, but, in spite of being patronized by the Royal Family, the pottery remained a quiet country concern until its closure in 1910. Wemyss Ware is perhaps the best known, and, with the exception of the early single-colored pots, the most readily identified line of ceramics ever to be made in Scotland. Production began in the Gallatown area of Kirkaldy in 1882, but it wasn't until the pottery's owner brought in Karel Nekola, an unusually gifted decorator from Bohemia, that Wemyss Ware began to feature the hand-painted flowers, fruit, animals, and birds for which it became famous. Nekola died in 1915 and, though the Fife pottery struggled on into the thirties, its later products lacked his original flair. Today, Wemyss Ware is the most sought-after of all Scottish pottery. **I**n Scotland as a whole, the ceramics industry collapsed in the aftermath of World War I due to the loss of export markets and changing social conditions. Despite the emergence of a craft movement, the industry has never recovered, leaving a rich and varied field for the collector.

LEFT, *a selection of Scottish spongeware kitchen bowls. Spongeware was much cheaper to produce than transferware, and was much more common.* ABOVE, *An early hand-painted Wemyss jug, thought to be the work of Wemyss master painter Karel Nekola, c. 1890.* OPPOSITE: *Examples of Scottish majolica, including a Montrose dog dish,* TOP, *a vase, two jugs, and an Alloa teapot,* BOTTOM LEFT. BOTTOM RIGHT, *another Alloa teapot and a water-lily jug.* OVERLEAF, COUNTERCLOCKWISE FROM TOP LEFT: *A green Wemyss pig, c. 1890–1930. Three small pigs, one painted with clover leaves. A honey jar and mug with a beehive motif. A ceramic basket and two large mugs decorated with cockerels are also thought to be the work of Karel Nekola. A Wemyss washstand set for Queen Victoria's Diamond Jubilee.*

A transfer-printed Caller Herring punch bowl, LEFT, showing East Coast fisherwomen with bonnets, long cloaks, and baskets of fish. Eight dinner plates and a meat dish, RIGHT, decorated with an item of Scottish regimental dress and a border of thistles. Made by Wedgwood in the early-nineteenth century, they reflect England's growing interest in Scotland.

CANKER

TON

Running out of houseroom at the farm, ABOVE, *the owner,* OPPOSITE, *is thinking of converting one of the old cattle-byres to take his "growing accumulation of stuff."*

The mysteries of scale are revealed at Cankerton, where what seems an impossibly spacious if low-ceilinged drawing room, ABOVE and BELOW, as well as a study, PREVIOUS PAGE, LEFT, and an ample dining room, RIGHT, all fit onto the ground floor of a small cottage.

A TYPICAL MID-EIGHTEENTH-CENTURY farmsteading, with a small cottage for the farmer wedged between the barns and byres that housed his livestock, Cankerton lies buried in the rich green dairy lands of North Ayrshire. Originally part of neighboring Blomridge Farm, the building had been allowed to fall into a ruinous state until it was restored in 1970 by a fox-hunting acquaintance of the present owner. "Beyond that, there's not a great deal to tell," he says, preempting any questions about the legendry of the house. "Cankerton isn't steeped in anything even approaching history. But I've lived here for twenty years. I'm devoted to the place. It's very central to all my activities, such as they are. Glasgow is only thirty minutes away by car, yet the setting could hardly be more rural." As Master of the Eglinton, the local hunt—a title he holds because "no one else would take on the job"—the owner has "view halloo-ed" over every hill and howe of the Lowland countryside. If the pursuit of the fox in southern Scotland seems somehow incongruous, raising the expectation that it might differ from the sport practiced in the English shires, he insists it is merely "Worse, but not different."

His countryman's knowledge of the area has been acquired over a lifetime. Born and brought up only three miles away at Rowallan, the neo-baronial mansion designed by the Edwardian architect Sir Robert Lorimer for his grandfather, the owner claims he bought Cankerton because of its handy proximity to his old home.

"Until it was sold the other day, I could always depend on getting free logs and the odd vegetable from the garden." The move allowed him to remain in the countryside he knows and loves, but the dramatic shrinking of accommodation from baronial pile to "but and ben" meant making adjustments. While the outside of the house has been preserved intact, a few internal walls were knocked down to give a nostalgic whiff of spaciousness, even grandeur. On the ground floor, the owner has managed to squeeze in a full complement of drawing room, dining room,

The owner's coat, ABOVE RIGHT, *which he wears as master of the local hunt, hangs among the various hats, boots, and saddles that occupy the "tack corner" of the bathroom, within easy reach of the front door,* ABOVE LEFT.

kitchen, tack room, and study without sacrificing comfort or spoiling the impression of surprising amplitude that is part of Cankerton's charm. Upstairs, two tiny guest bedrooms, with wood-lined ceilings so low that standing up suddenly can be hazardous, are a reminder of the true dimensions of the steading.

A few of the larger pieces of furniture, like the breakfront bookcase in the drawing room and a massive dining room sideboard, came from Rowallan. But the inspired jumble that fills every available corner of the house has been col-

lected over the years by the owner. From the Pre-Raphaelite drawings he bought for a song— "not even a song; a murmur, a chirrup"—while still at school, to the wistful portrait he found of Elizabeth Bibesco, daughter of the great Liberal prime minister Asquith, from the glass case displaying stuffed Scottish wildcats, to the field of 1950s painted-tin racehorses, there are things to surprise and delight the eye at every turn. The owner's informed eclectic taste has saved the cottage from completely overreaching its humble origins. An authority on Scotland's historic houses and gardens, he has also used a Buddhist's discretion in preserving the crop of dandelions and other weeds that fringe his domain. Nothing precious has been allowed to take root. In the book-crammed study hangs a portrait of the owner as a boy wearing a Cameron tartan kilt. By no means ashamed of his drop or two of Highland blood, the Master of Cankerton claims that he rarely finds the time or the occasion to wear a kilt, at least not in Ayrshire. "Too Lowland, too Lowland," he mutters into a brimming stirrup cup.

THE NORTHEAST

MAINS OF MA

YEN

Perched above the steep-sided Deveron valley, the old hall house of Mayen, OPPOSITE, and its newly made garden, ABOVE, with views of the winding river far below.

THE STEEP, WOODED VALLEY THROUGH which the River Deveron winds its way from Rothiemay to Marnoch has in its seclusive contours preserved something of the ancient Scotland. Prehistoric stone circles mar the even furrows of ploughed fields; early Christian gravestones stand or lie beside modern polished marble in the local churchyard. The immemorially cultivated landscape with its few isolated farms has hardly changed in three hundred years. High above the valley, where the Deveron takes a wide loop encircling the estate of Mayen, an old hall house commands the road, river, and surrounding hills. At dusk, the light from its narrow windows pricked out against the gathering darkness still promises, as it must have done in wilder days, a haven of warmth and security among the gaunt Banffshire uplands.

The cozily cluttered kitchen, RIGHT, *opens onto a walled herb garden at the back of the house,* ABOVE. *The owner's wife,* BELOW, *holding a lamb in the barn.*

The light, well-proportioned sitting room in the Victorian wing, ABOVE, has been decorated in appropriate period style. The bright glazes of Scottish majolica, RIGHT, are set off by pale apricot walls and deep red plush furniture.

The house of Old Mayen, which later became known as Mains of Mayen—"mains" is an east coast term for home farm—was built in 1680 over the remains of an earlier structure. A farming laird's small house, typical of Scots vernacular architecture in the sense that it was plainly and economically made by local men using local materials, its charm and interest now lie in the contrasts of scale between its modest size and massively thick, defensive walls. Like most tower and hall houses, built to withstand casual raids by marauding clans, cattle rustlers, or feuding

neighbors, Mayen had an outside first-floor entrance (now blocked off) that could only be reached by means of a retractable ladder. By the end of the seventeenth century, though, the emphasis had begun to shift from defensive austerity to convenience, comfort, and simple embellishments. Mayen's tiny stair tower in the reentrant angle between the two wings of the originally L-shaped building afforded protection, but also allowed such decorative flourishes as the fish-scale tiles on its pepper-pot roof and the carved plaque over the front-door lintel

bearing the owner's initials and coat-of-arms.

A hundred years or so after Mayen was built, the estate passed to the Duff family. Times had become more peaceful and it was no longer necessary for the laird to live in a fortified house. The prosperous Duffs abandoned the hilltop for a more picturesque site lower down the valley, where they built themselves an imposing Georgian mansion. The house of Old Mayen became home to the grieve, or farm manager, who in his turn abandoned the old Scots way of life and in 1840 added on a more dignified and comfortable wing. Mayen is still a working farm, though the present owners have created a garden where until recently only tractors and chickens cared to tread. Without major structural alterations, they have as far as possible restored the house to its plainer seventeenth-century incarnation—a now-fashionable destiny for many old Scottish houses.

There is no hint of Mayen's owners having succumbed to the fantasy of re-creating the Scottish Renaissance, which can lead the best-intentioned restorers astray. They have sensibly recognized that the rooms in the Victorian wing —light, well-proportioned, and appropriately decorated—make more spacious and convenient living quarters. But the spirit of the house still resides in the fortified seventeenth-century part, where family life revolves in clattery echoes about the turnpike stair, originally constructed so that it could be defended by one man and

The low-ceilinged dining room, RIGHT, *is in the original part of the house. Note the huge stone lintel over the fireplace and the old salt box built into the wall.*

threaded according to whether he held a sword in his right or left hand. Open a closet in any of the children's bedrooms and you are likely to find a turret temptingly provided with shot-holes. In the low-ceilinged dining room, a contemporary portrait of John Knox (the Scottish Luther) looks sternly down on oak furniture from England, while a wood fire burns cheerfully in a grate guarded by a pair of eighteenth-century French courtly figures. At Old Mayen, style and devotion to comfort firmly take precedence over the quest for authenticity.

The cluttered kitchen with its companionable Aga cooker, walls hung with pans, paintings, fishing creels, shelves full of collectible Scottish pottery, opens onto a walled herb garden at the back of the house. Once the front of the building, it formed with a stone dike and workers' bothy a half-made courtyard, which the present owners have squared off, paved, and filled with herbs and old-fashioned roses that are roughly the same date as the house (an example of period fidelity that could hardly be called overstated). The land to the southwest of Old Mayen has also been landscaped; terraces planted with mixed shrubs, roses, and herbaceous perennials now lead down from the fortified manor to a tiny but decorous summerhouse, a bucolic lookout on the edge of the fields with a strategic view of the Deveron cutting its wide silver arc six-hundred feet below and, on the far side of the valley, the dark hills rising.

LONG AFTER THE ENGLISH HAD ABAN-doned their medieval strongholds for more comfortable manor houses, the Scots (partly out of mistrust of the "auld enemy" south of the border) were still living behind battlements. In a chronically lawless country, ravaged by bloody feuds and grumbling war, defensive building afforded even peaceable lairds their only hope of security. Until the middle of the seventeenth century, the fortified stone tower remained Scotland's basic architectural form, evolving slowly and haphazardly from the crude Norman keep (erected in the Borders during the fourteenth century to repel both English and local raiders) to the soaring, multiturreted but essentially domesticated Jacobean tower house.

Descended remotely from the Iron Age broch, the early Scottish tower houses were built for passive defense wherever there was something, usually good agricultural land, worth defending. While the most powerful nobles lived in great castles of enclosure, which could provide security for an entire community, the lesser laird, his family, and the best of his livestock huddled together in the cramped quarters of what was effectively a vertical cottage. Uninhabited, yet perfectly preserved, Coxton Tower in Angus gives an idea of the grim realities of tower-house living. Constructed entirely of stone—even the roof tiles are thick slabs of granite—it consists of four tiny, vaulted rooms, one above the other, lit by narrow, un-

TOWER HOUSES

OPPOSITE, *a former Mackenzie stronghold on the Black Isle in Ross-shire, Kinkell was restored from a ruinous state in 1969 by sculptor Gerald Laing. Like all L-plan tower houses, its turnpike staircase is housed in a separate wing.*

glazed windows with wooden shutters to keep out the cold. The ground floor, or store, where the animals were crowded during a raid, has no access to the floors above other than a hatch in the center of the vaulted ceiling through which provisions could be drawn up. The entrance to the laird's living room on the second floor, where an open fire burned in the middle of the floor and the household conducted all its business in a funk of proximity, was reached by a ladder (later replaced by an exterior stone stair) that would have been pulled up at night or in times of danger.

Despite its late date, 1644, Coxton reverts to the oldest style of keep with its turnpike stair rising through the thickness of the walls to a parapet from which the tower could be defended.

Balfluig, a stark gray monolith rising out of the Aberdeenshire countryside, was built in 1556. An early L-plan tower house, its staircase is housed in a separate wing, which represents the first important departure from the four-square Norman keep. After the Battle of Arford in 1645, the tower was burned by Montrose, so effectively that its stone was still blackened when the present owner bought Balfluig in 1963 and began the work of restoration. As many as practical of the tower's original defensive features have been preserved. The owner's purist zeal succumbed only to Victorian sash windows in the great hall, which make this larger equivalent of the laird's room at Coxton a light, comfortable family space. It needs to be, for the other rooms at Balfluig are all head-bumpingly low and poky, from the vaulted kitchen to the caphouse at the very top of the tower, a tiny bedroom like the bridge of a ship with a 360-degree view of rolling farmland.

Of the three hundred or so surviving tower houses in Scotland, many are still inhabited, while others have regressed to little more than picturesque heaps of stone. But a growing number of these ruins (so evocative of the bad old days) are being saved, lovingly restored, and repossessed by born-again castle dwellers. Kinkell, built in 1549 by a chieftain of the Mackenzies, was rescued from dereliction by Gerald Laing, artist and sculptor, in 1969. Laing restored the tower, which had been gentrified in the eighteenth century (the gun loops plastered over or replaced with sash windows) to its original militant form. He made few compromises and was rewarded by the discovery that art and furniture of the twentieth century did not look out of place in the great hall. Tower houses, indeed, have the severe simplicity of modern apartments, but not the hidden space for the pipes and wires of modern conveniences. Visually demanding, they tolerate neither clutter nor shambles, but impose on their present-day occupants an orderly, inflexible, and somewhat self-conscious way of life.

Although Scotland's history continued in its turbulent course, by the early-seventeenth century the barons in their thrawn towers were be-

Tower houses range in style from the basic keep design of Coxton Tower, CENTER RIGHT, *to the Z-plan effusions of Craigievar, where the great hall has a fine early plaster ceiling,* BOTTOM CENTER *and* RIGHT. *Other examples include Hatton,*

CENTER, *Corgarff,* TOP RIGHT, *and Balfluig,* CENTER LEFT, *where an early L-plan tower is converted into as comfortable a house as the size of its rooms will allow,* TOP LEFT. *The foot of the turnpike stair at Kinkell,* ABOVE. *Window detail with coat of arms,* BOTTOM LEFT.

coming more interested in comfort and convenience than defense. As the need for physical strength in a building gradually declined, the domestic tower entered a period of transition from fortress to mansion house, becoming more elaborate, more softly commodious, while still retaining the authoritative, noble aspect of a castle. Initially, living space was increased by building upward rather than sideways; the parapet gave way to a roofline that over-sailed the wallhead as upperworks corbelled out over the top of the building. The towers grew wings (producing L-, Z-, and U-shaped plans), sprouted clusters of pepper-pot and angle turrets, bartizans, dormers, and balustrades. Thus, redundant martial features were adapted to serve the friendlier aims of architectural style.

Because of the political alliance between Scotland and France, it has often been suggested that only French influence can explain the dramatic exuberance and inspired fantasy, the splendid phallic grace of a Craigievar or Castle Fraser. But, while a certain Frenchness can be detected at Falkland and other Renaissance palaces, when it comes to domestic Jacobean tower houses, foreign influences are generally restricted to individual details. The imaginative uses to which they were put in these unique buildings is entirely native to Scotland and, reaching back to the earliest traditions of broch and tower building, represents the most characteristic and perhaps finest achievement of Scottish architecture.

A dashing young Jacobite, David Ogilvy of the Forty-Five, LEFT, escaped to France after Bonnie Prince Charlie's defeat at Culloden in 1746. Known as Le Bel Ecossais, he returned some thirty years later to reclaim his estates and live at Cortachy Castle, RIGHT.

CORTACHY

IN JUNE 1641, THE EARL OF ARGYLL DEscended on Angus with 5,000 men and a Parliamentary commission to lay waste the Royalist stronghold of Airlie Castle by "Fire and Sword." The assault was carefully timed to take place while the castle's owner, James Ogilvy, recently created Earl of Airlie for his family's loyalty to the Crown, was away at court. Argyll's fierce onslaught met with little opposition. According to "The Bonnie Hoose O'Airlie," a contemporary ballad, Argyll took up the hammer himself to help reduce the massive fortress to a pile of rubble. Meanwhile, Lady Airlie and her children had fled across the river to Cortachy Castle, an Ogilvy hunting lodge, which from that day to this has been the chief family home.

Although the older part of the house dates from the fourteenth century, there is no great sense of age about Cortachy. A vigorous hybrid of a building, it stands on the lush banks of the South Esk like a castle in a storybook, its cream-harled walls prettily relieved by features of dusky pink sandstone. The original tower looks austere enough, but the mainly nineteenth-century turrets and battlements have few martial pretensions. Cortachy was heavily baronialized in 1871 by David Bryce, a fashionable Victorian architect commissioned to add on a wing of thirty rooms, which was later demolished after the Second World War. While it may lack architectural distinction, Cortachy has a strong individual character. Seen at the end of the long beech avenue, or from across the river fields, the

The round tower at Cortachy, CENTER TOP, *seen at the end of the beech avenue,* TOP RIGHT, *finds an echo in the neobaronial gatehouse,* CENTER LEFT, *and an earlier, more sympathetic lodge,* BOTTOM RIGHT. *An Ogilvy family tradition of planting dedicated trees,* CENTER *and* TOP LEFT, *going back to the 1860s, has filled the park and gardens,* CENTER RIGHT, *with rare and beautiful specimens.*

tumbling rhythms of its gables and towers, catching the light and casting shade at oblique angles, create an impression of romance.

When HRH Princess Alexandra married the Honorable Angus Ogilvy, brother of the present thirteenth Earl of Airlie, she joined one of Scotland's most historic families, a family directly descended from the original Celtic earls of Angus, who were among the dynastic Seven Earls of Scotland. Celebrated in poetry and song, the Ogilvys have accumulated a wealth of legends, stories, and relics, many of them relating to Cortachy. The castle wears its history lightly, but there is no denying the thrill of finding Charles II's prayer book in the room where he slept and of learning how he had left it behind in his hurry to escape his Covenanting minders. In a corner of the dining room, the trapdoor by which the king got away remains in working order, though the connecting tunnel to the far side of the river has since been filled. On a side table, crystal glasses engraved with a symbolic white cockade were once tacitly used to drink the health of Stewart kings "over the water."

The most romantic figure in the family story, David Ogilvy of the Forty-Five, would certainly have drunk from them. After eloping with his wife, Margaret, at the age of sixteen, the twelfth Lord Ogilvy was packed off to a military academy in France. A dashing young Jacobite, known as *Le Bel Ecossais* at the French court, he was inspired by Prince Charles Edward to return home in the summer of 1745 and raise the

Ogilvy regiment in his support. David shared the early successes of the Forty-Five Rebellion and, at the triumphant ball at the Palace of Holyroodhouse in Edinburgh, Lady Ogilvy was given the honor of leading the first dance with the prince. The dress she wore for the occasion, one of Cortachy's most poignant Jacobite relics, seems small enough for a child. David survived the Battle of Culloden and escaped to France, where he remained in exile until pardoned in 1778. Margaret, who was caught trying to escape and briefly imprisoned, joined him at Versailles but returned periodically to Scotland to give birth to their children, having granted her husband the permission he politely requested to take a mistress. When at last he came back to Cortachy, dressed as a colonel in the French army and with French manners and an ineradicable accent, David quietly resumed the life of a local laird and set about restoring his estates.

If the spirit of *Le Bel Ecossais* lingers on at Cortachy, the signs of French influence have disappeared long since. The older furniture in the castle is solidly Dutch, which was then the fashion of neccessity even among prominent families living north of Kinross. Rarely able to afford the spoils of a grand tour, they relied on trade with the Low Countries to furbish up their houses. When Blanche, the first English-born Countess of Airlie, arrived at Cortachy in the 1860s, she was appalled by how uncivilized life there was and wasted no time in putting matters right. A formidably ambitious Whig lady, she

The drawing room at Cortachy, LEFT, *shows the influence of the Victorian architect David Bryce. A painting of Airlie Castle, the Ogilvy family seat until 1641, hangs over the hall table,* ABOVE. *A writing desk in a quiet, sunny corner of Cortachy,* BELOW.

The present Lady Airlie's sitting room, ABOVE, *where the ghostly Airlie Drum sits unceremoniously on the floor. A collection of early pottery,* LEFT, *some of it bearing Blanche Airlie's monogram.*

had plans for baronializing Airlie Castle (modestly renovated by Ogilvy of the Forty-Five), but had to be satisfied instead with leaving her stamp on Cortachy. It was her notion to throw out the Bryce wing—Blanche insisted it include a ballroom—and though little remains of the Victorian extension, the force of her grand ideas can still be felt about the house, not least in the now rather touching plethora of BA monograms on everything from breadbins to the weather vane.

There are no ghosts at Cortachy, only the remains of the Airlie Drum, which lie unceremoniously in a corner of the present Lady Airlie's sitting room. The story goes that before Argyll attacked in 1641, he sent a drummer-boy to deliver an ultimatum. The Ogilvys replied by taking the boy hostage. They encased him in the drum and left him suspended from a turret, the Dummer's Tower, where he died still drumming on the inside of his instrument. A curse was laid on the family that whenever an Earl of Airlie was about to die, the drum would be heard again. The rat-a-tat-tat of impending doom last sounded in 1900, when the Lord Airlie of the day was killed in the Boer War, while at Cortachy, thousands of miles away, Lady Airlie among others distinctly heard drumming.

The vaulted kitchens at Cortachy, PREVIOUS PAGE, show the immense thickness of the castle walls. A bedroom in the Bryce wing, ABOVE, compared with smaller bedrooms in the older part of the castle, LEFT and BOTTOM, reveals the Victorians' need for more civilized living. A piece of silk embroidery, BELOW, worked by Lady Blanche Airlie.

A gathering of kilts in Lord Ogilvy's dressing room, LEFT. The silk dress, BELOW RIGHT, worn by Ogilvy of the Forty-Five's wife, Margaret, NEAR RIGHT, when she opened the ball at the Palace of Holyroodhouse with Bonnie Prince Charlie, is one of Cortachy's most romantic Jacobite relics. A ball program, FAR RIGHT, of more recent vintage lists many forgotten reels. A set of pottery, CENTER RIGHT, fills a window niche.

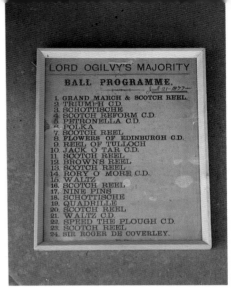

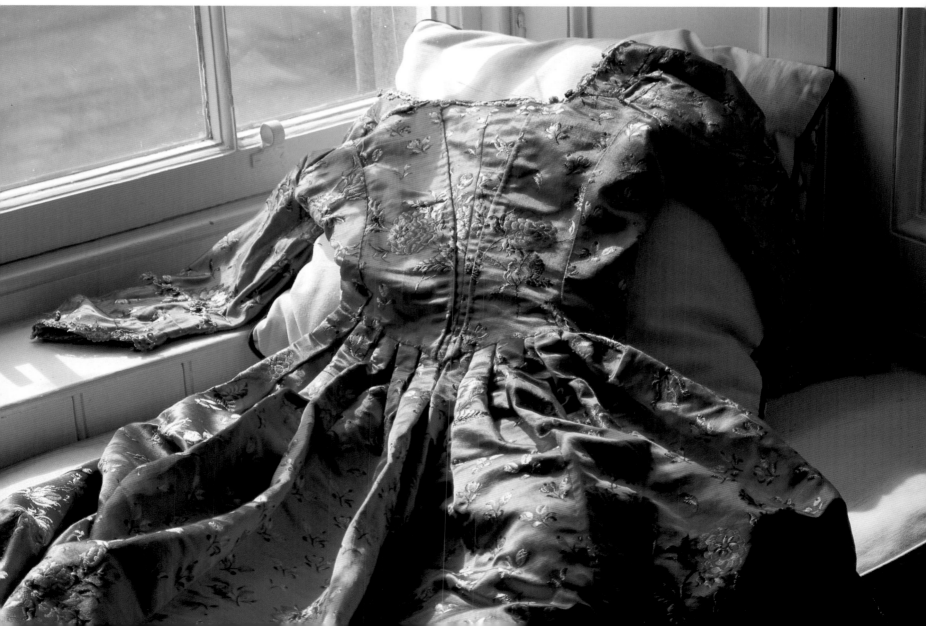

THE ROMANTIC IMAGE

IMAGINE A HOST OF BONNIE PRINCE Charlie and Flora Macdonald look-alikes, dripping in tartan, endlessly dancing whisky-quickened reels in the damp moonlight to the approving hoots of loyal clansmen. . . . The Brigadoon Complex, one might call it, if only these heart-catching images ever faded instead of remaining as bright and firmly fixed in the popular imagination as the lid on a box of shortbread. It's a picture of Scotland, originated by the poets and writers of the Romantic age, that for over two hundred years no amount of sobering reality has been able to dispel. The fuddled legends of Scottish history, still a recognizable influence on Scottish life, and the stirring beauty of the countryside both serve to nurture a sentimental fallacy, which, long recognized by Scots (not altogether cynically) as a source of national pride and revenue, has kept Caledonia forever wreathed in the mists and myths of its own creation. The single most important source for this rhapsodic view of Scotland is the fraudulent but nonetheless stirring poetry of Ossian. The apparent outpourings of a third-century west coast bard, discovered and "translated" from the Gaelic by James Macpherson (1736–1796), their authenticity was challenged by Dr. Johnson, who showed that, although loosely based on fragments of Celtic lore, the poems were Macpherson's own compositions. Their dubious provenance, however, did not prevent Ossian from catching the imagination of all Europe, es-

OPPOSITE, *detail,* Glencoe *by Horatio McCulloch, from 1864.*

pecially Germany. The epic of Fingal became one of the most admired and imitated works of the Romantic movement, inspiring Goethe, Johann Herder, and, later, Felix Mendelssohn, who made a pilgrimage to Fingal's Cave on Staffa to experience the wave-swept locale for his haunting *Hebrides* overture. Ossianic fever brought the first trickle of tourists to Scotland. Their enthusiastic accounts of dramatic scenery and hospitable natives outweighed the appalling discomforts of travel in the north and made the Highlands and islands an irresistibly exotic destination. Not all the early travelers, however, were equally impressed. Dr. Johnson, whose *A Journey to the Western Islands of Scotland* (1775) was famously scathing about the country and its inhabitants, observed that: "The finest prospect a Scotsman will ever behold is the highroad that leads to England." But in an age that worshiped nature and exalted the noble savage, there was no halting the approving fashion for the elemental grandeur of Scotland's landscapes and the simple dignity of the warm-hearted, heroic folk who lived in its glens—a fashion that our nation's two greatest writers would soon turn into an industry. Besides spreading Scotland's fame abroad, Robert Burns and Sir Walter Scott helped to create a new romantic image of Scotland, which, however idealized, returned to the Scottish people a sense of their own identity and a self-respect that, since the union with England and the failure of the Jacobite rebellions, had

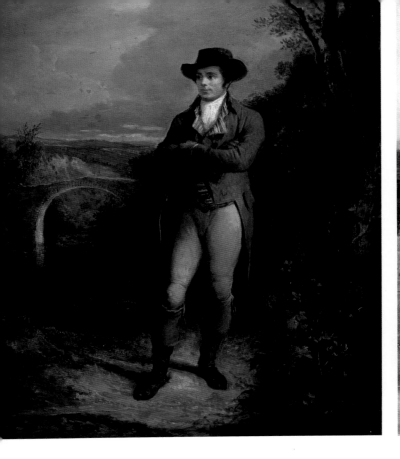

AE FOND KISS, AND THEN WE SEVER;
AE FAREWELL, AND THEN, FOR EVER!
DEEP IN HEART-WRUNG TEARS I'LL PLEDGE THEE,
WARRING SIGHS AND GROANS I'LL WAGE THEE.
WHO SHALL SAY THAT FORTUNE GRIEVES HIM,
WHILE THE STAR OF HOPE SHE LEAVES HIM?

ME, NAE CHEERFU' TWINKLE LIGHTS ME:
DARK DESPAIR AROUND BENIGHTS ME.

I'LL NE'ER BLAME MY PARTIAL FANCY,
NAETHING COULD RESIST MY NANCY!
BUT TO SEE HER WAS TO LOVE HER;
LOVE BUT HER, AND LOVE FOR EVER.
HAD WE NEVER LOV'D SAE KINDLY,
HAD WE NEVER LOV'D SAE BLINDLY,
NEVER MET—OR NEVER PARTED—
WE HAD NE'ER BEEN BROKEN-HEARTED.

ROBERT BURNS
FROM *AE FOND KISS*

sunk to a low ebb. A popular romantic hero himself, Robert Burns was the handsome, philandering son of a ploughman who wrote poetry of genius and died young. He reinterpreted Scotland to the Scots, celebrating their humanity in a language of tolerance that allowed his countrymen to see themselves again as "men o' pairts"—great drinkers, great lovers, bonnie fighters both for freedom and the rights of man, and, the frailty of triumph and failure notwithstanding, as "men for a' that." If Burns restored to the Scots their virility and self-confidence, Sir Walter Scott gave them back their history. Not the harsh reality of bloodstained centuries, but a colorfully dramatic pageant, in which the hero-figures of Robert the Bruce, Mary Queen of

Scots, Rob Roy, and Bonnie Prince Charlie were given a mythical status that has kept them bathed in the glow of the Celtic twilight ever since. This was a Scotland that all Scots could justly feel proud of and identify with in healing retrospection. To the rest of the world, Sir Walter Scott's idealized portrayal of Scottish landscape and Scottish history, its violence safely enshrined in the gloried past, gave Scotland an iconic glamour that nineteenth-century artists from Thomas Duncan and Allan Stewart to Landseer and Horatio McCulloch ensured it would never lose. The enormous success of Scott's narrative poems and, later, the Waverley novels, brought waves of tourists north of the border. They came to drink in and shed tears

A painting of Dalzell, near Hamilton, 1835, ABOVE NEAR LEFT, *by Horatio McCulloch, 1805–67. An emotional response to the Scottish landscape was cultivated by the poets Robert Burns, 1759–96, painted by Alexander Nasmyth,* ABOVE FAR LEFT, *and Sir Walter Scott, 1771–1832, by Sir Henry Raeburn,* ABOVE. *Antonio David's idealized 1732 portrait of Prince Charles Edward Stewart,* ABOVE RIGHT, *has never faded in the popular imagination.* Scottish National Portrait Gallery *(above near left, above, and above right).*

over the scenery described in *The Lay of the Last Minstrel* and *The Lady of the Lake,* and to marvel at the sublime settings of *Rob Roy* and *Redgauntlet.* But they came too to pay homage to a world-famous author and much-loved public figure. Only Scott, the Wizard of the North, could reconcile recovering the Scottish regalia, a sad reminder of Scotland's lost independence, with arranging the 1822 state visit to Scotland of George IV, the Hanoverian king he presented, tartan-wrapped, to the Highland clans. In a sense it all comes together in Abbotsford, the neobaronial mansion that Scott, the self-created Border laird, literally dreamed into existence on the proceeds of his fiction. An extravagant assemblage of medieval towers, crow-stepped ga-

bles, and cloistered gardens, every detail of its construction informed by vivid antiquarian fantasy, Abbotsford has been unkindly described as Scott's finest historical novel. But the house personifies the generous, cosmopolitan spirit of the poet and of the Romantic age in Scotland. It united Scott's love of the heroic past with a more enlightened view of the present, balancing tradition with progress (Abbotsford was one of the first houses to be lit by gas), modern furnishings with a fantastical collection of Scottish relics (gleaming armor, heraldic shields, grim battlefield trove), and domestic comfort with the first revival of the ancient Scottish baronial style, which was to have such an important influence on the development of Victorian taste. The Romantic image of Scotland that Sir Walter Scott so tirelessly promoted was given the ultimate

Romantic views of Loch Lomond, ABOVE, *and Loch Achray at sundown,* OPPOSITE TOP, *both painted by Horatio McCulloch in the 1860s.* OPPOSITE BOTTOM, *a watercolor by Carl Haag of Queen Victoria and Prince Albert enjoying a Highland picnic at Carn Lochan c. 1862–65.*

seal of approval by Queen Victoria's extended love-affair with the Highlands. The baronializing of Balmoral, both as architecture and in its interior decoration, set a fashion followed by Scottish lairds as faithfully as by the English industrialists who emulated them on their new Highland sporting estates. In a sense, the royal family's continuing enthusiasm for things Scottish has kept up the work that Ossian, Burns, and Scott began: to preserve Scottish traditions and give the Scots a welcome, if somewhat dubious, mythic identity. Abroad and at home, nostalgic Scots perpetuated the myths of a land that bore little relation to the Scotland they knew or remembered, reliving in painting, poetry, and songs a history that may have been part fantasy, but that nurtured the enchantment of belonging now petrified in the national consciousness.

THE HOUSE OF M

ONYMUSK

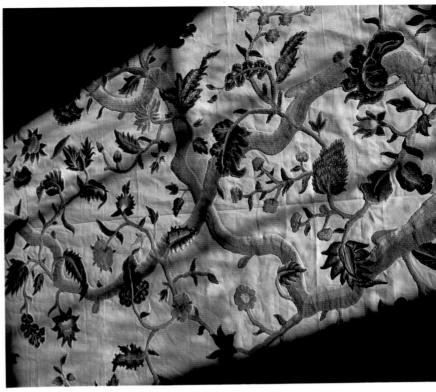

THE YEAR AFTER ROBERT THE BRUCE'S victory over the English at Bannockburn in 1314, a small jeweled casket shaped like a house, and containing relics of St. Columba, traditionally paraded in front of Scots armies before they went into battle, was given into the keeping of Malcolm de Monymusk by the Abbot of Arbroath. There is no record of why the seventh-century "Brecbannock" or Monymusk Reliquary, as it came to be known, changed hands. The abbot, Bernard de Linton, may have believed the reliquary would be safer behind the strong towers and barmekin walls of Monymusk than at Arbroath Abbey, where six years later he was to formulate the defiant Declaration of Arbroath. A letter to the Pope protesting Robert the Bruce's excommunication, signed and sealed

Over the years, the House of Monymusk, PREVIOUS PAGE LEFT AND RIGHT, has been extended and rebuilt without losing its character, as an early-nineteenth-century painting shows. The circular shape of a turret room, ABOVE LEFT, makes an ideal small library. The fine seventeenth-century tapestries, ABOVE RIGHT and OPPOSITE RIGHT, representing the Tree of Life and other allegorical subjects, were embroidered by Lady Anne Forbes of Monymusk.

by the barons, clergy, and commons of Scotland, the Declaration stated unequivocally: "For so long as a hundred of us are left alive, we will yield in no least way to English dominion. We fight not for glory nor wealth nor for honours: but only and alone we fight for freedom, which no good man surrenders but with his life."

While Scotland's fortunes over the next six hundred years fluctuated, to say the least, the Brecbannock remained secure at Monymusk, surviving the house's several changes of ownership and political allegiance, but not the vagaries of Estate Duty. In 1930, the Monymusk Reliquary was reluctantly sold by the present laird's grandfather to the Museum of Antiquities in Edinburgh. Still a matter of contention with the family, the departed reliquary had repre-

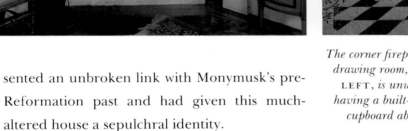

The corner fireplace in the drawing room, ABOVE LEFT, *is unusual in having a built-in china cupboard above it.*

sented an unbroken link with Monymusk's pre-Reformation past and had given this much-altered house a sepulchral identity.

Some form of monastic foundation had probably existed at Monymusk since the time of St. Ninian, the first of the great missionaries to proselytize Scotland. The now-vanished Augustine priory of Monymusk, built in the twelfth century, was originally a house of the Culdees, the secular Servants of God who spread the word of the Celtic church through their exemplary lives. By the mid-sixteenth century, however, the lives of their descendants had become less than edifying. In 1554, Monymusk Priory, insolvent and dissolute, was destroyed by fire, and its prior arrested while celebrating divine service in Aberdeen Cathedral, charged with arson, theft, assault, adultery, and murder. The priory lands were later sold to the Forbes family, a powerful local clan, who used stones from the ruined religious buildings to construct an L-plan tower house about the remnants of the original castle.

An architectural mongrel, the House of Monymusk has been extended and rebuilt so often over the centuries that it would defy classification were its irregularities not typical of many Scottish baronial houses. As early as 1716, it was described deploringly by its new owner, Sir Archibald Grant, as "an old castle with battlements, six different roofs of various heights and directions, confusedly and inconveniently combined and all rotten." His own improvements and a much later Victorian wing added to the

99

roofs—and the confusion. But in its lush pastoral setting, a fertile valley below Paradise Woods on the banks of the river Don, this rambling, attractively awkward, pink-harled "castle" makes up in atmosphere what it lacks in stylistic distinction. Inside the house, a labyrinth of narrow passages and twisting stairs connects one period of its history to another. A visitor may wander from the baronial great hall with its painted beams and the arms of James VI of Scotland above a huge open fireplace; cross the parquet of a Victorian drawing room; descend a turnpike stair to a stone-vaulted store at the foot of a medieval tower with a well in the middle of the floor; then climb another tower to emerge unexpectedly amid the classical harmonies of what is oddly enough the only gloomy room in the house, an eighteenth-century library, lined with leather-bound books, maps, and family portraits.

The largest and handsomest of these portraits shows Sir Francis Grant, Lord Cullen, surrounded by his wife and children, soon after he bought Monymusk in 1712 from its Forbes owners, who had fallen on hard times. (The present laird, Sir Archibald Grant, thirteenth baronet, recently married a Forbes, which gives a pleasing symmetry to the destiny of the house.) As a prominent Whig and Judge of the Court of Sessions, Lord Cullen had helped draw up the unpopular 1707 Act of Union between Scotland and England—an ironic credential that must

An eighteenth-century engraving of Monymusk, BELOW, *with the River Don in the foreground.* RIGHT, *the white and gold drawing room runs the length of the Victorian wing.*

An aumbray, OVERLEAF LEFT, *beside the fireplace in the great hall may once have housed the communion host. The Forbes arms painted onto the wall are "three bear's heads muzzled." The eighteenth-century library at the top of the house,* OVERLEAF RIGHT, *is dominated by portraits of the Grant family, who acquired Monymusk in 1712. The room may well be haunted, but in daylight hours the present Sir Archibald Grant has no reservations about going up there.*

100

have rattled the bones of St. Columba inside the Monymusk Reliquary. Lord Cullen never liked the house, but handed it over to his eldest son, Archibald, who immediately began the transformation of the estate that brought him fame as one of the great pioneers of agricultural improvement. A friend of "Turnip" Townsend, the English agricultural reformer, Sir Archibald enclosed the arable land at Monymusk, converting a "wild and dreary moor" into fields bearing a variety of crops. He planted trees (fifty million of them over a long life), built roads, houses, and schools and encouraged his tenants to follow his revolutionary methods by sending them packets of turnip seeds for Christmas. An unsparingly energetic man, who married four times (outliving three of his wives), he wrote disparagingly about the second Lady Grant, formerly Anne Potts: "My wife is a dreadful Slug-a-bed, 'tis oft six of a morning ere she rises."

Standing in front of the porch on a warm spring day, I asked the present Lady Grant, the very antithesis of a slug-a-bed, if the House of Monymusk was haunted. "I've never seen any ghost," she answered carefully, "but in an old place like this you don't tend to look for them. I mean after ten o'clock at night we would never dream of going up to the library. When we're alone, sitting in the room below, we often hear footsteps. You learn to live with that sort of thing without feeling obliged to investigate."

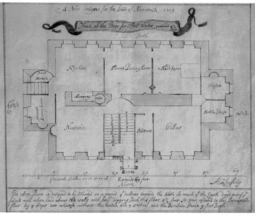

The great hall, now the dining room, LEFT, has retained its baronial spirit, emphasized by the stags' heads and a display of armor, TOP. The coat of arms of James VI of Scotland and I of England are painted over the huge fireplace. Some of the ceiling beams are also painted. A plan of the house, ABOVE.

105

THE DISCOVERY OF A REMARKABLE SERIES of painted Renaissance ceilings in the great Jacobean tower of Crathes in 1877 must have seemed a dramatic revelation. Exposed during alteration work under a preservative covering of Georgian plaster, the ceilings disproved a popular misconception. Far from having grim bare interiors, the houses of well-to-do Scots in the sixteenth and seventeenth centuries were resplendent with bright colors and elaborate design. A peculiarly Scottish phenomenon—domestic painted ceilings are rarely found in England, emphasizing the lack of contact between the two countries at the time—there is little doubt that this elemental style of decoration was imported from Northern Europe. The plump blondes and bearded warriors of the ceilings at Crathes have a somber, unmistakably Teutonic air, suggesting the cultural influence of Scotland's main trading partners across the North Sea in Scandinavia and the Low Countries. There are clear affinities with similar decorative work in places like Gripsholm, Vadstena, or Runkelstein in the Tyrol, but the evidence points to the artists themselves being Scots tutored in foreign techniques and inspired perhaps by imported pattern-books. Scottish painted decoration dates roughly from 1570 to 1650. A medieval tradition, the painting of walls and ceilings was originally associated only with religious buildings. When the Reformation brought the decoration of churches to an abrupt

PAINTED CEILINGS

Uncovered in the nineteenth century, the painted ceiling in the chapel at Stobhall, dated 1642, shows the mounted kings of Europe, OPPOSITE *and* OVERLEAF TOP, *as well as the Drummond coat of arms and reclining stag.*

halt in 1560, it left craftsmen free to apply their art in the houses of nobles and merchants. The stylistic homogeneity of many Scottish ceilings suggests that individual artists or family groups of artists may have traveled the country to find commissions. Skills were passed on from father to son until the demand for painted ceilings was overtaken by the new fashion for ornamental plasterwork, which reached Scotland in the mid-seventeenth century. The chapel at Stobhall, a partly medieval courtyard house in Pertshire, contains one of the most unusual painted ceilings in Scotland. Like the ceilings at Crathes, it was uncovered in the nineteenth century, when its background colors of pale blue, fawn, and white were partially repainted, though the figures and the Drummond coat of arms were left untouched. Designed for what was originally a secular room, the ceiling is thought to have been painted in 1642 and depicts the contemporary mounted kings of Europe with their armorial devices as well as such legendary figures as Prester John. Realistic rather than allegorical—the King of Mauritania is shown riding an elephant—the primitive representations in clean, vibrant colors create a festive overall design that complements their part-domestic part-ecclesiastical setting. Ceiling painting was a slow, meticulous business. It could only be carried out after the ceiling was in place, obliging the artists to work above their heads. With the simpler type of open ceiling found at Crathes and Stobhall, designs

had to follow the beam-and-plank formation of the floor of the room above. The exposed timber, and in some cases stone or plaster work, was painted over with a variety of patterns displaying birds, animals, biblical or mythological scenes, heraldic emblems, or instructive mottoes. The artists generally drew out their designs before filling in the colors, producing a matte but luminous painting with a durable tempera finish. The inscriptions in black Gothic script

Domestic painted ceilings, rarely found in England, were a Scottish phenomenon lasting a hundred years. Designs following the beam-and-plank formation of the floor above at Pinkie House, BELOW LEFT, *and Crathes Castle,* BELOW RIGHT. *The remains of a frieze,* BELOW CENTER.

were added last and, in accord with the contemporary taste for the pious and proverbial, included such whimsical Latin tags as: "It is a husband's fault when a wife overspends his income." Another surface that lent itself to painted decoration was the barrel-vaulted timber ceiling; one of the bedrooms at the Palace, Culross, a small sixteenth-century merchant's house on the shores of the Firth of Forth, provides a fine example with charmingly intimate

allegorical illustrations. Coved ceilings offered an uninterrupted expanse allowing freer, more sophisticated designs that the viewer could take in as a whole. The 78 foot–long ceiling of the painted gallery at Pinkie House, Musselburgh, attempts (not altogether successfully) to create a trompe l'oeil cupola as its centerpiece. An intricate, ambitious work, it took several years to complete (the artist is said to have died of exhaustion the day it was finished) and represents

Vaulted timber ceilings provided a larger canvas, allowing the artist greater freedom of expression as in the painted gallery at Pinkie House, ABOVE, *and a bedroom at the Palace, Culross,* BELOW CENTER *and* RIGHT. *Arguably, the more naive designs at Crathes,* BELOW LEFT, *were more effective.*

the culmination of a soon-to-be outmoded tradition. When compared to the contemporary paintings and frescoes of the late Renaissance in Italy, the decorated ceilings of Scotland seem crude and naive indeed. Yet the artistic cheerfulness, the unaffected delight in the novelty of adornment that they display marked an important departure from the rough simplicity (not to say appalling discomfort) of Scottish domestic life before the Reformation.

The Queen Mother, LEFT, stands in the doorway of her Scottish home, Birkhall. The garden, RIGHT, sloping away below the house, is where the Queen Mother spends as much time as possible when she's at Birkhall.

BIRKHALL

DERIVING ITS NAME FROM THE SILVER birch trees that grow around the house, Birkhall stands on its own green plateau overlooking a secluded garden bounded by the River Muick and the wooded hills of Royal Deeside. Over the years several additions have been made to the original Queen Anne house, built of Aberdeen granite by a local Jacobite family in 1715. But the white-harled walls and gray-slated roof have knit the building together so harmoniously that it has become difficult to tell old from new. Only the wooden porch, supported by four oak trunks, stripped of their bark but with the stumps of their branches left protruding to give a rustic effect, is obviously Victorian and a reminder that Balmoral lies within walking distance. The porch stands out gaily from the whiteness of the house and, festooned with hanging baskets of geraniums, creates an impression of homely comfort and welcoming openness.

Queen Elizabeth The Queen Mother describes Birkhall as "A small big house, or a big small house." Whichever you prefer, it is certainly on quite a different scale to the great castle of Glamis where she grew up, not as a royal princess yet destined to add the first truly Scottish dimension to the Crown since the Stewarts. After the death of her husband, George VI, in 1952, the Queen Mother was given Birkhall by her daughter, the present Queen, enabling her to return to a house that she had grown to know and love as Duchess of York. Before the Duke

In the entrance hall, BELOW, *Queen Elizabeth's collection of pale blue gardening coats stands out against the tartan wallpaper. A small army of corgis gathers here at mealtimes,* RIGHT, *to be fed. Every square inch of stair and passage walls,* LEFT, *is covered by* Spy *cartoons.*

succeeded to the throne, following the abdication of Edward VIII, she had spent many happy summers there with her family. At the bottom of the garden stands a thatched "Wendy House," where years ago the Princesses Elizabeth and Margaret used to give make-believe tea parties. Having already begun to put her inimitable stamp on the house and garden, it was with some regret that Her Majesty gave up Birkhall's informal charm for Balmoral. Over the last thirty years, however, she has made Birkhall wholly hers again: a place of peace and enjoyment, where she can indulge her love of the Scottish countryside and her lifelong interest in gardening.

A high wall of cypress flanks the house to the left of the porch, acting as a windbreak to the herbaceous borders along its southern face and giving the terrace a sheltered, private feeling. The sunken garden, lying some fifty feet below and only visible from the edge of the lawn, comes as a munificent surprise. An old-fashioned garden of common varieties, it favors annuals and roses that flower either early or late in the season to coincide with the Queen Mother's May and August visits. In the traditional Scottish way, flowers and vegetables grow side by side. The borders, lined with white heather hedges, are neatly laid out in the shape of a bell, but with an abundance of plants in bloom spilling over the paths and making gentle mockery of the formal design. A green gazebo stands at the top of the rockery, the highest point in the garden,

BELOW, *a sampler map of Balmoral Forest.* OPPOSITE: *A modest eighteenth-century laird's house, added to over the years,* Birkhall, LEFT AND RIGHT CENTER, *was originally bought by Queen Victoria for her son, Edward VII. The green gazebo at the top of the rockery,* BOTTOM LEFT,

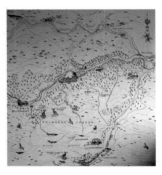

offers a quiet place to sit and enjoy the views of the Dee valley. A thatched "Wendy House," TOP CENTER, *where years ago the royal princesses gave tea parties. Flowers, fruit, and vegetables grow together in mixed borders creating the atmosphere of an old-fashioned cottage garden. A mass of* Phlox paniculata, BOTTOM CENTER, *lines the steps leading up to the house.*

where the Queen Mother likes to sit with her dogs and enjoy the views of the Dee valley and the moors beyond.

The spirit of the garden pervades the house. The drawing room in the new wing opens onto the terrace and is kept as full of flowers as a conservatory. Light and airy, with bow windows that overlook the river, it has an informal atmosphere. In a corner under a painting by Edward Seago stands an old upright piano—a reminder that the Queen Mother, like all her family, is musical; singing has always been a part of life at Birkhall. As impressively run as any royal household—the equerries come and go, policemen disguised as gillies patrol the grounds, a silver tray full of dog bowls appears on the porch at precisely the corgis' feeding times—what makes Birkhall a warm, lively place are the personal, mildly eccentric touches: the stack of "Fawlty Towers" videos, the eleven grandfather clocks the Queen Mother gathered together in the dining room "because it seemed rather amusing, at the time," the hundreds of framed *Spy* cartoons that cover the stair and passage walls.

All signed by their subjects, the *Spy* cartoons were originally collected by Sir Dighton Probyn, the Queen's Keeper of the Privy Purse, who lived at Birkhall in the 1890s. They date back to the beginnings of *Vanity Fair* and include, in its "Men of the Day" series, a caricature of Edward VII, for whom Birkhall was bought in 1849 by his mother Queen Victoria. Not sharing her obsession with Scotland, the Prince of Wales stayed only once at Birkhall, finding the house small and uncomfortable. It was later reappropriated by Queen Victoria, who filled it with friends, courtiers, and, on one occasion, the subject of another *Spy* cartoon, Florence Nightingale.

The Queen Mother comes to Birkhall every spring and summer; in September she moves up to her second Scottish home, the Castle of Mey on the remote coast of Caithness. At Birkhall, more than anywhere, she can be herself, potter .about the garden in old clothes, take her small army of dogs for walks, and have her family and friends to stay. She continues to enjoy the country freedoms and typically outdoor pursuits of her Highland childhood. Guests sent out fishing, shooting, or stalking are expected to report to Her Majesty (a skilled fisherwoman who only recently gave up fishing the Dee) how they got on over a leisurely picnic lunch. Picnics are the order of the day, every day, much as they were in Victorian times. Lunch, Queen Elizabeth The Queen Mother will explain, is not a meal to be eaten indoors. Born with the century, the first genuinely Scottish link with the royal tradition of summering in Scotland, she owes her enormous popularity to the public perception that she embodies the best of the Scottish character, drawing her natural warmth, strength, and inspiration from her native countryside.

RIGHT, *The Queen Mother entertains family and friends with a picnic lunch by the banks of the River Dee.*

A MEASURE OF ANY GARDEN'S CHARM IS its capacity to surprise. Finding Arduaine, a woodland garden on a rugged promontory that looks out over the Sound of Jura is like stumbling on a lost Eden. Beyond the garden gate, as if the climate itself had suddenly changed, one enters a subtropical haven of lush lawns, rare trees, and enormous flowering shrubs that fill the warm salt air with their scent. It may be the nature of great Scottish gardens to seem unexpected, but the shock of discovering a corner of Burma, palm trees and all, in the West Highlands, of glimpsing a collection of Italian garden statuary on a misty Hebridean isle, or of coming across bonsai growing outdoors by the barren coast of Wester Ross, only adds to the explorer's delight in these remote, unspoiled places. Scotland took to gardening relatively late in its history. The vanished herb terraces of the Beatons, hereditary witches to the Lords of the Isles, may have been the first planned gardens, but the earliest known garden plans date only from the sixteenth century. Characteristically, the Scots soon caught up, and, over the last two hundred years, have managed to produce against the odds some of the world's most inspirational gardens and gardening pioneers. Meeting the challenge of wild country and unreliable weather, early gardeners turned the brief Scottish summer to account by building walled gardens that stood against biting winds, cornered the sun's rays, and fulfilled the imperative need of tender

GARDENS

▪▪▪▪▪▪▪▪▪▪▪▪▪▪▪▪▪▪▪▪▪▪▪▪▪▪▪

Under a rampant specimen of Rhododendron rubiginosum, *horticulturalists Edmund and Harry Wright,* OPPOSITE, *the brothers who spent twenty years restoring the Argyllshire garden of Arduaine.*

plants for shelter. The walled kitchen garden, designed to intensify the short growing season, might be described as an essentially Scottish arrangement. Often lying behind the grim redoubts of fortified houses or, in Victorian times, at a respectful distance from the big house, it established a tradition of vegetables and flowers growing side by side in democratic profusion. At Logan Botanic Garden on the Mull of Galloway, cabbage palms and tree ferns now flourish within the temperate precincts of what was once a traditional walled garden. Three hundred miles further north, the old kitchen garden at Dundonnel has become home to a unique collection of exotic plants without losing its original character. The line between ornament and simple function in Scottish gardens has always been appealingly vague. On the west coast, mild winters, due to the warming influence of the Gulf Stream, acid soil, and plentiful rain, provide ideal conditions for creating woodland gardens. In the nineteenth century, Scots who had been abroad in the service of the British Empire experimented with bringing back local flora from its far-flung corners. A consortium of lairds and industrialists paid for expeditions of plant-hunting botanists to recover species from China, the Himalayas, Upper Burma, and New Zealand. The plants thrived in Scotland and, regenerating as easily as they did in their original habitats, soon looked as if they had been growing there forever. Arduaine, one of Argyll's

Looking out over the Sound of Jura to a misty prospect of western isles, RIGHT, Arduaine benefits from the warming influence of the Gulf Stream, which allows tender plants, ABOVE, to thrive in subtropical conditions.

most romantic gardens, was begun in 1898 by James Arthur Campbell, a Ceylon tea planter, who shipped seed back from the Far East in tea chests and achieved some notable successes, including the first flowering in the Western hemisphere of *Rhododendron giganteum*. Arduaine remained in Campbell hands for three generations until 1971, when the much-neglected garden was taken on by Edmund and Harry Wright, horticulturalist brothers from England, who lovingly restored it to its former glory. The bleak terrain, scarcity of level ground, and somewhat overpowering scenery in Scotland discouraged the kind of formal landscaping developed by Capability Brown and others south of the border. Scottish gardeners dealt with the problem of the competing backdrop in a variety of ways. Early efforts, like the seventeenth-century parterre at Drummond, private and

The highland glen garden at Crarae, started by Sir George Campbell seventy years ago, continues to flourish under the care of his son, Sir Ilay, FAR LEFT, who shares his father's gift for using form and color in the garden with the vision of a "painter in plants." Dramatic views of Loch Fyne, LEFT, through stands of Tasmanian snow gums, Chinese rhododendrons, and Pennsylvanian cherry trees.

inward-looking, simply ignored the dramatic views around them. But as architects grew more confident, so did their attempts to relate house and garden to the countryside. One of the first landscapers was Sir William Bruce, who sited Kinross House (pages 38–47) so that its focus on the romantic ruin of Loch Leven Castle might engage the formal garden with its natural setting. From there developed the ultimately more refined and demanding relationship, perhaps Scotland's greatest gardening achievement, between wild gardens and wild nature. **C**rarae, a steep highland glen on the shores of Loch Fyne, could easily be mistaken for a ravine in the foothills of the Himalayas. The long climb up the side of a rushing burn is rewarded by views of hill and loch with the advantage of being able to see plants from above and below as one walks. There are surprises at every turn—a Himalayan magnolia glowing through a clearing like a tree of light bulbs, a carpet of wild violets and bluebells in a grove of Tasmanian snow gums, bloodred species of Chinese rhododendron growing beside cherry trees from Pennsylvania. **S**ir George Campbell started to develop the main glen garden at Crarae in 1925. Once described as a "painter in plants," he disclaimed artistic gifts, insisting that he never landscaped or designed the garden, just let it happen. But the subtle orchestration of leaf, flower, and form on such a grand scale could hardly have been accidental. Sir George's son, Ilay, who inherited Crarae and the responsibility for keeping one of

Scotland's great gardens going, stresses the importance of the rare and beautiful trees his father planted as a canopy to shelter tender plants. The danger on the west coast, where the common *R. ponticum* grows like a takeover bid from a hostile planet, is that gardens tend to become collections of rhododendron species. At Crarae, the Campbells have been careful not to let rhodies swamp other, less showy shrubs and trees, though Sir Ilay, who possesses his father's flair for choosing the right plant for the right spot, claims to be less concerned about "what something is than what it looks like. The *effect* of a garden is all that really matters." On a cliff above Loch Etive, the woodland garden at Achnacloich starts close to the house. Established about 1860, when the estate belonged to kinsmen of Robert Louis Stevenson, the garden, as it is today, was mostly laid out by Jane Nelson and her late husband, Ernest, who had been inspired as a boy by his uncle, the celebrated plantsman F. R. S. Balfour. Protected by a fringe of tall Scots pine and larch, it slopes southward between two natural ridges in a series of hillocks and dells crossed by paths and, where water flows, wooden bridges. Arresting views of Mull and Ben Cruachan from scattered lookout points give the policies an unusual feeling of openness. Yet it remains an intimate, poetic garden, full of private corners, where one can enjoy a haunting fragrance, a particularly fine specimen, or the drowsy hum of a half-wild place. "I like a garden with nothing much in it," says Jane

A carpet of daffodils and narcissus stretches away in front of the house at Achnacloich, ABOVE. *Trees were cleared to open up views of the surrounding hills, leaving a fringe of larch and Scots pine to protect the garden's intimate corners,* RIGHT, *where rare species grow in a half-wild setting.*

Nelson. "I hate the feeling of being smothered in plants that don't look as if they belong. It can be very exhausting." The peaceful bounty of Scotland's wild gardens makes it easy to forget the hard work and imaginative daring that created them. Plants brought back from wildernesses abroad were committed to no-less-virgin ground at home and nourished with blind faith and patience. Osgood Mackenzie, who in 1862

A bluebell glade meets a wall of rhododendron in the woodland garden, ABOVE, behind Logan Botanic Garden on the Mull of Galloway, the most southerly part of Scotland.

built his famous garden at Inverewe on bare rock, had to wait fifteen years for pine shelter belts to grow before he could even start planting. A tough pioneering spirit put at the service of rare and exotic beauty reflects the paradoxical Scots character. The names of Balfour, Forrest, Forsyth, Douglas, Cox, and many others, found on botanical labels all over the world, are a reminder of the extraordinary contribution to

horticulture made by Scotsmen. Intrepid, driven, often eccentric personalities, they endured appalling hardships on collecting expeditions to the very ends of the earth. "It is only Scots dourness which carries me on," George Forrest wrote home on his 1904–06 trip to China, from which he brought back rare species of primula that are now as much a part of the Scottish woodland scene as bluebells.

Logan enjoys a mild climate year-round, allowing a rare diversity of plants, ABOVE, *to thrive in the open air that would otherwise need glasshouse protection. Looking out over palm trees and rhodies,* RIGHT, *to the Solway Firth.*

THE WESTERN ISLES

C A M

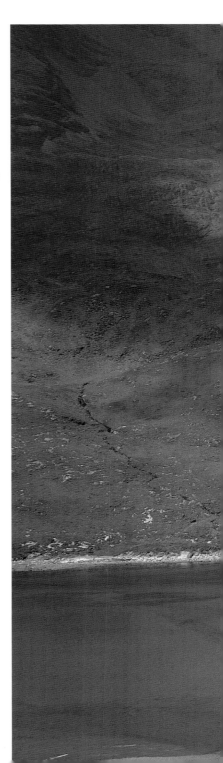

A far fishing lodge on the isle of Skye, RIGHT, *Camasunary can only be reached by boat or on foot. Traced "portraits,"* LEFT, *are made of all sea trout weighing over eight pounds caught at Camasunary.*

ASUNARY

IF THERE'S A PLACE WHERE FLY-FISHERMEN go when they die, then it's likely to have been inspired by Camasunary, a fishing lodge on the island of Skye that lies like many a vision of paradise in its own lush, well-watered glen surrounded by inhospitable mountains. Getting there entails "a ninety-minute plod," as Alan and Louise Johnson, the owners of the lodge, lightly put it, across the back of the Elgol peninsula. When at last you breast the pass under Ben Meabost, any reserves of breath are taken from you by a daunting first glimpse of the Promised Land. At five miles range, rain and mist permitting, the Black Cuillin rear up, jaggedly vigilant, a dragon's comb of gabbro and basalt peaks looming over the half-hidden valley and looking out across the Cuillin Sound to the Small Isles. A long way below, Atlantic rollers beat in on the white sandy beach at the head of Loch Scavaig, the faint smell of seaweed growing stronger as you climb down toward a strip of wind-shorn pasture dotted with sheep, the refuse of winter storms and ruins of a long-deserted crofting village. A hundred yards back from the shore, in the green midst of this sequestered wilderness, stands the house at Camasunary.

Originally part of the Strathaird estate, Camasunary was bought by Alan Johnson's great-grandfather from McEwen of Eigg, a wandering laird whose frequent travels in the Far East earned him, on Skye at least, the reputation of an opium smuggler. When Alan was first taken to Camasunary as a boy, the land was still being

The Johnson family, BELOW NEAR RIGHT, *returning from a fishing expedition. Meals are eaten in a corner of the lodge living room,* RIGHT, *pictured in a watercolor by Emma Tennant,* BELOW FAR RIGHT, *who also painted the view of the Cuillin hills.*

132

farmed; now, apart from a few summering sheep and backpackers, the glen stays empty most of the year. Beyond the farmhouse, where the Johnsons live when they come to fish, there is a small bothy known as "The Celtic," which they have made available as an overnight shelter for mountain climbers. The Cuillin Ridge, towering three thousand feet above Camasunary, has been attracting mountaineers and sightseers since the early-nineteenth century. At one time, every British landscape artist of note, including Turner, felt obliged to paint Loch Coruisk (darkly celebrated in Sir Walter Scott's *Lord of the Isles*) as a Highland scene of supernatural gloom, all beetling crags and lowering skies, but bearing little resemblance—in summer anyway —to Coruisk's banks and bonny blue waters where only the fishing is out of this world.

When they move to Camasunary (usually between June and October), the Johnsons bring all their supplies with them, either by boat or in a landrover inched over the pass. In the fishing season, they can expect to live off what they catch setting pots for lobster and langoustine around the bay skerries, gathering mussels and scallops along the shore and taking sea trout and a rare salmon from the freshwater lochs. The house provides all necessary comforts: stove, hot water, refrigerator, and, downstairs only, gas lighting—a candle lights you to bed. In the living room, the accumulation of paperbacks and board games suggests years of wet afternoons and long evenings by the fire. Overlaying the well-worn furniture, an existential jumble of fishing tackle, game books, and stray bits of equipment—an outboard engine in one corner, a pile of rainbow-hued chiffon scarves knotted into "midge veils" in another, and, on a high shelf, an ancient box of permanganate marked "For Adder Bites"—leaves no doubt that life at Camasunary is mostly lived outdoors.

Around the yellowing wood-lined walls, portraits of significant sea trout caught in the three lochs (Creitheach, Athain, and Coruisk) swim

The nearby lochs once teamed with prize trout, but their numbers have declined in recent years, which is perhaps why the fish haven't yet reached the bedrooms, ABOVE RIGHT.

nose to tail all through the house. Known as "moonies," once-in-a-blue-moon fish that tip the scales at over eight pounds, they are not so much trophies as tributes to honored adversaries. It's a Camasunary tradition—no one can remember how or when it got started—that whoever catches a moonie has to paint its portrait. First the outline of the fish must be traced onto stiff paper (a box of old wallpapers in the attic serves the purpose), then cut out and used as a stencil, so that regardless of the artist's skill the size of the fish will be accurately recorded. Some of the older portraits have begun to fade, but they make a lively and varied collection, revealing perhaps more about the people who painted them—"They do tend to have worryingly human eyes," observes Louise Johnson—than the individuality of the fish. One or two were painted by well-known artists, but their efforts cannot be said to stand out from the shoal.

There have been no moonies caught at Camasunary since 1985, when a mysterious decline in sea trout stocks was first recorded on the west coast of Scotland. Alan Johnson believes that the numbers have been falling off for more than a decade, almost certainly as a result of environmental pollution. While mourning the big fish and the pristine wilderness he knew as a boy—"People and rubbish seem to be on the increase," he says, "everything else keeps getting rarer"—he has no fears of Camasunary's secluded character becoming spoiled. Looking back from the top of the pass, you can see the lazy-beds where a community once raised crops and, further up the glen, the depleted peat hags that forced the crofters to abandon their homes. The hills still bear witness, but there are few wild places in the Highlands that do not reverberate with human associations. Every year, the Johnsons will tell you, they receive puzzling compliments from strangers coming off the Cuillin on the fine bed of potatoes growing over by "The Celtic," where the land has not been cultivated this century.

The barren moonscape of
South Harris seems an
uninviting spot to put down
roots. But, looking out to
sea, Flodabay House,
LEFT, *enjoys magnificent
views and a peaceful
hinterland of wilderness.
Digging up peat to fuel
winter fires,* RIGHT, *is a
traditional summer activity
on Harris.*

FLODABAY

FACING THE SEA, FLODABAY HOUSE stands with its back to a wilderness only a little less desolate than the surface of the moon. The hills that rise gently behind the house are not high, but they are as barren as mountain crags with patches of vegetation clinging on here and there between bald outcrops of stone. A modest, two-story wooden building without architectural pretensions, the house was built in the 1970s for its present occupants by a local contractor. As best they could, they kept the structure in sympathy with its surroundings, using grayish tiles on the roof that would blend in with the rocky landscape; now, the darker house timbers have begun to weather to the same gray color. Camouflaged, set back from the narrow, coastal track that winds around the Bays of Harris—the Golden Road, as it was ironically dubbed by inhabitants of the few scattered hamlets it serves—the position of the house in the landscape remains nonetheless uncompromising, almost defiant in the face of the elements.

"In the Hebrides, the loss of an inhabitant leaves a lasting vacuity," Dr. Johnson observed in 1775, "for nobody born in other parts of the world will choose this country for his residence." When they first moved to Harris, the English-born occupants of Flodabay were the exception that proves the rule. Dr. Johnson, though strongly prejudiced against Scotland, was often exasperatingly right: The story of the Hebrides has been one of both gradual and (in the case of unscrupulous nineteenth-century landlords

The artist's study, TOP LEFT, *reveals a lifetime's passion for birds—even sea gulls,* TOP CENTER. *A once keen falconer, he painted the goshawk,* TOP RIGHT. *The green sea cliff,* BOTTOM RIGHT, *hidden behind the offshore island of Scarp, provides nesting places for thousands of birds in spring. St. Clements Church at Rodel,* CENTER LEFT, *contains one of the finest sixteenth-century tombs in Scotland. The remote bothy,* CENTER RIGHT, *where the owners sometimes spend a night on a fishing or stalking expedition. Peats laid out to dry,* BOTTOM LEFT. *The rugged terrain of Harris,* BOTTOM CENTER, *softened by flowers.*

clearing the islands of people to make room for sheep) rapid depopulation. Yet, in recent years, the tide has been stemmed if not quite reversed by immigration. In spite of the discouraging climate, the remoteness, the material disadvantages of living in the Outer Isles, there has been a small but steady influx of "white settlers," as the locals call them, bent on escaping the overcrowded conditions of the south. Some stay long enough to put down roots, like the thriving community of Gaelic-speaking Pakistanis in Stornoway, others last only a few winters before scurrying back to civilization.

"We came to live here," says the owner of Flodabay, who has known and loved Harris since he was a child, "because we wanted a simple outdoors life, freedom, solitude, the challenge of being somewhat self-sufficient." His wife concurs, but quietly points out that it might be misleading to describe life at Flodabay as simple. When she goes shopping (for all but basic necessities), it means driving to Stornoway, a two-and-a-half-hour round-trip. In summer, she grows vegetables in "lazy-beds"—the hand-dug plots that the islanders have wrested from the grudging earth for centuries—and has managed to create a small miracle of a garden among the rocks and the ruined walls of an old black house. The growing season is cruelly short, but she gets a sense of satisfaction from working within its limitations, following the rhythms of island living. Like every family on Harris, the "incomers" work their own peat hags

and make sure they dig and dry enough peats in the summer months to keep them warm through the winter. On an island bare of trees, the only available firewood is what can be picked up on the beaches. When the weather closes in they can find themselves housebound for days, sometimes weeks, on end.

The interior of Flodabay has the comfortable atmosphere of a sea-going yacht decorated in the style of an English country house. The family possessions reflect a long connection with the Royal Navy. Everywhere there are mementos of life at sea: brass telescopes, engravings of sloops and men-of-war, shell collections, wall-charts and sextants, a treasured letter from Admiral Nelson. For several years, the owner worked as an independent commercial fisherman, living with his wife in a tiny, now abandoned, crofting village on the offshore island of Scarp—an existence so isolated it makes the Bays of Harris seem metropolitan. Although the fishing venture came to an end, boating still plays an important part in their lives; there's always a Zodiac inflatable on a trailer parked outside the house, ready to be launched at a moment's notice.

An artist and naturalist, the owner now makes his living painting birds and leading summer visitors on bird-watching expeditions around the islands. The Hebrides are a paradise for ornithologists. Migrant and native species like the eagle, plover, and red-throated diver share the vastness of a northern sky that at mid-summer

A lone standing stone, ABOVE, *on the west coast of Harris —immovable evidence that the island has been inhabited since the Stone Age. A view of island hills,* BELOW. *The house is full of references to the sea, including a letter from Admiral Nelson,* PREVIOUS PAGE CENTER, *and a ship of the Mediterranean fleet,* RIGHT, *commanded by one of the owner's ancestors.*

HANNIBAL 91 CAPTAIN FARQUHAR REAR ADMIRAL RODNEY MUNDY . C.B
SECOND IN COMMAND IN MEDITERRANEAN
1859 1860 1861

never darkens. Because the landscape affords them so little cover, birds are rewardingly visible; they nest on the ground, in plain sight. Where superstitions linger on among the old people, unearthly significance is still read into their comings and goings. Birds are recognized as part of life here, warily welcomed—like tourists—as transient members of the community.

Once the owner fostered a golden eagle that had been found covered in fulmar oil and unable to fly. He nursed it back to health and kept

The garden at Flodabay, ABOVE *and* RIGHT, *finding what shelter it can among the rocks and ruined walls of an old black house, has to make the most of a short growing season.*

it at home for a couple of years before returning it to the wild. The eagle's portrait has pride of place in the kitchen at Flodabay, an indication perhaps of the value the family places on living in close harmony with the natural world. Behind the house, the eagle's offspring can sometimes be seen in rough weather circling over the barren heights, hunting the moorland and fishing the black, peaty lochans, which can turn in an instant to silver and brilliant blue under the swiftly changing skies.

THE WORD *TWEED* DERIVES FROM AN error by a London clerk who, making out an invoice in 1826, wrote *tweeds* instead of *tweels*, a Scots rendering of *twills*. Orders were placed for more "Scottish tweeds." The novel description of the coarse woolen cloth caught the public's imagination, and soon became established in the clothing trade as a quality brand, the itchy but authentic uniform of the country gentleman. It is sometimes said that Scottish tweed, to qualify as "the genuine article," should come from the Outer Hebrides. Individual preferences aside, nothing could be further from the truth. Some of the finest, most expensive, as well as most popular, tweeds are woven in factories and small local mills all over Scotland. There can be no doubt, though, that the making of Harris Tweed, the most internationally renowned of all Highland cottage industries, is confined by law to the Outer Hebrides. The protection by trademark of perhaps the only textile in the world whose methods of production are dictated by geographical and social considerations rather than market efficiency gives Harris Tweed a certain cachet. Long before the *Clo Mor*, or "big cloth," became known to the world as Harris Tweed, it was standard wear in every crofting community of the Hebrides, where its warmth, durability, and resistance to rain and shrinkage were ideally

TWEED

The small, hardy blackface sheep, OPPOSITE, *once an interloper, is now seen everywhere in the Highlands and Islands. The making of tweed affirmed the crofter's self-sufficiency, providing work for the long winter months.*

suited to the harsh island climate. The cloth was traditionally made at home by seasonal processes involving the crofter's whole family. Once the sheep had been sheared in late summer, the wool would be steeped in natural dyes distilled from heather, lichens, and wildflowers usually gathered by children. During the long winter evenings, the women carded and spun the wool into yarn, which was then woven into cloth on wooden hand-looms by the men. Come spring, the tweed was ready for the finishing process of fulling or waulking—a communal activity in which the women sang in Gaelic as they worked, rhythmically thumping the soaked cloth and improvising verses about most aspects of island life. In 1840, Lady Dunmore, the wife of the proprietor of Harris, recognizing the quality of the cloth the islanders made for their own use, determined to find a wider market for "Harris" tweed and bring money into the island's subsistence economy. Among her English friends, she promoted the subtly shaded tweeds that blended in with the hills from which they were taken as the ideal wear for stalking, shooting, and fishing. Dressing up in the local costume not only helped them get into the spirit of things, but was a practical way of protecting themselves from the elements. Tried and tested by the islanders, the hillman's rough cloth soon acquired a nubbly

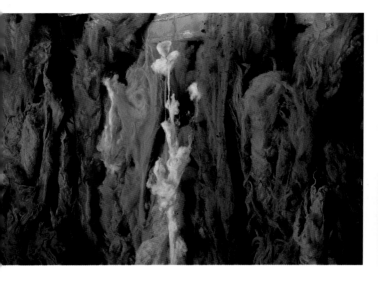

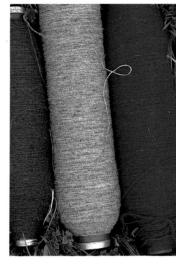

mystique, which it has never quite lost. **U**nder Lady Dunmore's resolute patronage, the demand for Harris Tweed grew, benefiting the islanders but making the old ways of production impractical: the market required patterns that could be accurately repeated. This meant the design of the tweeds had to be standardized and the wool dyed and spun in mills rather than in

On Harris, Catherine Macdonald, OPPOSITE TOP CENTER, *spins her own wool, colored with natural dyes boiled up in a pot over a peat fire. Alisdair Campbell,* BELOW LEFT, *demonstrates the semimechanized Hattersley loom, while his aunt, Marion Campbell,* BELOW RIGHT, *works at a traditional wooden hand loom.*

crofters' outhouses. The communal aspect of tweed production was nonetheless kept alive by the efforts of the Harris Tweed Association, founded in 1909, to protect the industry and its craftsmen. A somewhat eccentric system now prevails whereby the yarn is delivered to self-employed weavers on the islands of Harris, Lewis, the Uists and Barra, allowing them to

work at home in their own time and on their own looms. Once woven, the cloth is collected from the weavers' houses (recognizable by the bales of tweed lying outside in all weathers), and brought back to the factories to be finished and stamped with the Harris Tweed orb trademark. **P**urists would say the cost of standardization has been too high, robbing the tweed of its idiosyn-

The finished product purveyed by James Campbell, "Tweed Mercer," BELOW RIGHT, *at Campbells of Beauly, which stocks a variety of tweeds from mills all over Scotland. Regular customers include King Hussein of Jordan and actor Charlton Heston, as well as locals, who can have the tweed made up by a tailor on the premises.*

cratic nature. Among the older people there are still a few who dye their own wool in cauldrons of crotal, marsh marigold, and iris, who spin their own yarn, and work the wooden hand-loom that produces a softer, thicker, living cloth —the *real* Harris Tweed. Hearteningly, they have full order-books and growing numbers of disciples.

QUIDNI

In her converted black house at Finsbay, South Harris, OPPOSITE and ABOVE, Rachel Morrison does not miss the lack of modern conveniences, though without television or radio, she admits life can be "too peaceful at times."

THE JOURNEY TO THE OUTER HEBRIDES, which lie some fifty miles west of the Scottish mainland, can either be halcyon or dismayingly rough depending on the mood of the North Minch. According to legend, the "Blue Men" of this notoriously fickle sea rise up and challenge sailors to complete a half-written line of verse before deciding whether or not they will survive the passage. If you're a good enough poet to make it across, you are likely to appreciate that there is nowhere on earth quite as beautiful. A tapering pelagic skeleton of land, pounded the length of its western flank by green Atlantic breakers, the Long Island (as the Outer Isles are collectively known) offers empty miles of silver shell-sand beaches backed with flat grasslands and desolate peat moors.

This ancient country littered with incidental monuments and megalithic riddles—the great stone circle at Callanish on Lewis rivals Stonehenge in mystery and beauty—has a rich heritage of history and legend kept alive by the Celtic tradition of storytelling and ancestral pride. One of the last strongholds of the Gaelic language, the islands and their crofting communities retain a strong sense of their own identity, a thriving musical and poetic culture, and a way of life that has always depended on the remoteness of the Hebrides for its survival.

Until the end of the Second World War, as many as half the croft houses in Outer Hebrides were based on the indigenous black house design that more than any other style of Scottish

building defines and represents the human character of the Highlands and Islands. Only a few black houses are still inhabited, and most of these—like Rachel Morrison's snug cottage at Quidnish in South Harris—are conversions. The older houses have either been pulled down, found use as cattle-byres and peat stores, or left roofless to crumble. In the crofting townships, they stand beside the modern bungalows that replaced them like destitute relations. Yet, while a certain stigma still attaches to its "primitiveness," the black house has come to be recognized as an architectural success story.

In a region where no trees grow, where the wind blows unrelentingly, where rain falls two days out of three, the black house was designed to withstand the rigors of the climate. Low to the ground, its streamlined shape gave it the sheltering look of an overturned boat. Its immensely thick walls were packed with a mixture of peat and gravel for insulation. The rounded thatch roof, held in place by ropes made of twisted heather weighted down by stones, reached only to the inner wall, leaving no eaves to be caught by the wind. Rainwater drained into the cavity material between the walls, keeping it moist and draft-proof. A small hole in the roof allowed some light to penetrate and smoke to escape from the peat fire kept going day and night on a central hearth; it was from the dark, soot-blackened, smoky interior that the black house took its name. Every spring the islanders stripped off the sooty thatch and used it to fer-

tilize their crops. Manure collected through the winter from livestock that shared the same roof was kept indoors, out of the leaching rain. Today, black house living would be given the Green seal of approval as an ecologically sound, self-sustaining system. Improvers of the Victorian age, however, shocked by the apparent lack of hygiene, pitied the islanders living "in hovels like animals," failing to see that these warm, dry houses made healthy and comfortable homes.

At Quidnish, Rachel Morrison's improved "white" cottage, with its stone chimneys and brave new windows imposed on an earlier black house, probably dates from the late-nineteenth century. Over the windows, the eaves of the painted corrugated iron roof, a more recent innovation, have been cut back (leaving the guttering momentarily suspended) to let more daylight infiltrate the four-foot thickness of the walls. Rachel remembers that when her husband was alive and they worked the croft, the roof was still made of thatch, which they would strip each spring and lay on the potato beds in the traditional way. She does not miss the inconveniences of the old style of life; yet she considers herself better housed now than many who live in modern cottages that "feel" the wind. There is something satisfying as well as reassuring about thick walls encompassing a small space. A cozier, more congruous interior than the living room of Rachel's croft would be hard to find. But an exaggerated sense of security is characteristic of Scottish architecture, which has always depended for its effect on a combination of pleasing proportions and massiveness, whether in the baronial turrets of Culzean Castle or in the rubble walls and keel-shaped roof of a black house ploughing the stormy Hebridean skies.

THE HIGHLANDS

On its rocky peninsula overlooking Loch Crinan, Duntrune's formidable defenses, RIGHT, enclose surprisingly small living quarters. One of the oldest inhabited castles in Scotland, it has belonged to the Malcolms of Poltalloch since the late-eighteenth century. As the wife of a working farmer, Suzy Malcolm, LEFT, gets up early to feed her flock.

DUNTRUNE

ON THE NORTH AND WILDER SHORE OF Loch Crinan, Duntrune Castle stands splendidly isolated on its own rocky promontory commanding what was once an important sea-route from the Western Isles (by way of Loch Awe) to the central Highlands. Its dramatic position, rising almost sheer from the sea and looking out across the Sound of Jura to the ship-swallowing Corryvreckan whirlpool, gives Duntrune an impressive force, an air of sullen impregnability, only somewhat mitigated by its relatively small size for a medieval fortress. One of the few surviving examples of the Norman-influenced stone castles that first appeared in Scotland in the twelfth century, Duntrune has been rebuilt several times over the past eight hundred years, but its foundations and the massive curtain wall girding its outer defenses date from that period and

The castle walls, ABOVE LEFT, *growing out of the rocks, are often battered by storms. "The sound of the waves against the castle of Duntrune" is a well-known pipe tune. The castle's forbidding appearance has been softened by such Victorian details as monogrammed guttering,* ABOVE CENTER, *and stags stop gateposts,* ABOVE RIGHT, *salvaged from the demolished Poltalloch House nearby.*

lend some credence to its claim to be the oldest continuously inhabited castle in Scotland.

Curiously, for such an ancient structure, it has very little recorded history. The earliest known reference to Duntrune makes no mention of who built the original castle, or when; it states merely that Duncan Campbell, whose father Cailean Mor supported King Robert the Bruce's claim to the Scottish throne, had a royal charter of "Duntroon." A longtime Campbell stronghold (the majority of castles in Argyll were controlled by the Campbells), Duntrune thereafter remains lost in its west coast mists until the mid-seventeenth century, when a celebrated incident saved the Castle of Turrets, as it was known then, from almost certain destruction.

In 1645, an Irish adventurer called Coll Macdonnel landed on the Mull of Kintyre with three

thousand men and marched northward, plundering and pillaging as he went. When he reached Crinan, Coll sent his piper ahead to spy out the land and determine the strength of the castle. The piper managed to gain admittance to Duntrune, but soon aroused the suspicions of his Campbell hosts, who locked him up in one of the turrets. Impatient of waiting, Coll Macdonnel had by now ordered his ships to advance up Loch Crinan. When the piper saw them sailing into what he knew was a trap, he played a tune from his turret window warning that he had been taken prisoner and advising his chief against attacking the strongly defended castle. On hearing the tune—a *piobraich* known to this day as "The Piper's Warning to His Master"—Coll turned his ships around and sailed away, leaving Duntrune unscathed. The Campbells,

Inside the courtyard, the L-shaped dwelling house, ABOVE LEFT, *was built in the sixteenth century over the remains of an older house. The doocot,* ABOVE CENTER, *with its curved roof was restored by Robin Malcolm's father. Looking out through the main entrance,* ABOVE RIGHT, *across the Crinan Moss.*

realizing how they had been tricked, seized the piper and only put him to death after they had hacked off both his hands. For years afterward, the piper's spirit was believed to haunt Duntrune, where phantom pipes could often be heard wailing from the turrets.

The story might have ended there but for a curious archaeological discovery. In 1792, Duntrune was sold by the Campbells to their neighbors, the Malcolms of Poltalloch, an old Argyllshire family who lived across the Crinan Moss at Kilmartin. In the late-nineteenth century, the Malcolms let Duntrune to an Episcopal minister, during whose tenancy the castle dwelling house, an L-plan Jacobean tower incorporating a much older structure, was damaged by fire. While repairs and alterations were being carried out, an alcove was revealed behind some

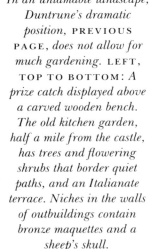

In an untamable landscape, Duntrune's dramatic position, PREVIOUS PAGE, does not allow for much gardening. LEFT, TOP TO BOTTOM: A prize catch displayed above a carved wooden bench. The old kitchen garden, half a mile from the castle, has trees and flowering shrubs that border quiet paths, and an Italianate terrace. Niches in the walls of outbuildings contain bronze maquettes and a sheep's skull.

old paneling; inside it, the workmen found the skeleton of a man without hands. The tenant was asked by his landlord to give what were assumed to be the piper's remains a Christian burial and to "lay his spirit" with the ancient rite of Bell, Book, and Candle. After this was done, it was said, the ghost of the Macdonnel piper was never seen or heard again.

The Malcolms only came to live at Duntrune after the present owner's father demolished nearby Poltalloch House, an enormous, unmanageably grand Victorian mansion that had been the family seat since 1850. Before moving into the castle in 1959, the late Colonel Malcolm, Chief of Clan Malcolm and, incidentally, grandson of the famous Edwardian beauty Lillie Langtry, refurbished Duntrune's austere living quarters, placing the emphasis firmly on comfort—his wife insisted on a modern kitchen and bathrooms—but without sacrificing the integrity of the building. The original front door and spiral stairs were abandoned for a more sheltered entrance from inside the courtyard; the old kitchen on the same floor was converted into a bedroom and dining room (now used as a study); and, upstairs, the Jacobean great hall high above the rocks became a bright aerie of a drawing room with reflected light from the loch washing into the room on three sides and dancing the gloom out of the bare stone walls.

There are days when the wind blows so fiercely it's hard to stand up in the castle precincts, when horizontal rain lashes the battle-

LEFT, *on the vaulted ground floor of the castle, the kitchen looks out onto the flagged courtyard. The snug heart of the house, warmed by the constantly burning Aga stove, it's where the Malcolms eat and their working dogs sleep, each in its own inalienable corner.*

ments and the crash of the waves breaking against the curtain wall makes conversation indoors an effort. Living in a fortress on the west coast of Scotland, even a pocket-size fortress like Duntrune, is probably not for the fainthearted. As a working farmer, Robin Malcolm, the present laird, finds the castle on its lone promontory less practical than the farmhouse he lived in before he inherited the estate and certainly more costly to maintain. But he and his wife, Suzy, who have made Duntrune as cheerful and unassuming as its ancient fabric and atmosphere will allow, consider themselves fortunate to be its custodians. They have never been unduly troubled by drafts or by ghosts. Only when pressed will they admit to rare occasions—not always on a dark, dripping winter's night— when, sitting by the stove in the study, their three dogs have suddenly started barking at the arched window embrasure, which used to be the entrance when the castle was fortified, baring their teeth and raising their hackles at an unseen visitor.

RIGHT, TOP TO BOTTOM: *The Jacobean great hall high above the rocks has been converted into a comfortable drawing room. In the study, built up from a once-open courtyard, family portraits stand out against white plastered stone walls that are at least six-feet thick. The rampant stag and an Orkney chair seem inalienably Scottish.* LEFT, *Robin Malcolm's dressing room with kilt laid out on the bed and piano ready for a reel.*

ONE OF THE STRANGEST DEVICES IN Apollo 11's moon-bound cargo, proudly worn by astronaut Neil Armstrong at the moment of taking his first "giant leap for mankind," was a strip of his own tartan. Now on display at the Museum of Scottish Tartans in Comrie, the moon exhibit illustrates both the heroic and the irrational strands woven into the motley story of Highland dress. With the possible exception of whisky, no national emblem of Scotland has a wider, more emotive appeal than tartan. Yet its mystique largely rests on a popular fallacy that clan or family tartans are as ancient as the hills, when in reality the great majority were invented by the Victorians, to whose voguish enthusiasm for the Highlands tartan probably owes its survival. The kilt, most distinctive of all tartan apparel, is still worn in Scotland (chiefly in the Highlands), not with the self-consciousness of national dress, but no longer altogether casually. Although a practical and comfortable alternative to trousers outdoors, the kilt has evolved into an expensive form of Sunday best or evening wear and bears little resemblance to the original garb of the Highlander. This, the belted plaid, was nothing more than a rough piece of cloth sixteen-feet long by five-feet wide that was donned by lying down on top of the gathered plaid (it served as a blanket at night) and belting it on. The wearer then stood up, trailing a long unpleated tail that could either be looped over his left shoulder (leaving his sword arm free) or

TARTAN

The origins of tartan, from the French tartaine, *are obscure and the subject of endless controversy. Some of the best-known clan tartans may be little more than a hundred years old. Yet few would dispute the importance of the tartan motif and of Highland dress in the history and sentiments of the Scottish people. A portrait of Flora Macdonald,* OPPOSITE, *by Richard Wilson, 1747 (Scottish National Portrait Gallery), next to the Lennox tartan.*

used as a cloak. The modern "little kilt" or *philabeg,* a less cumbersome but not so versatile garment, only came into general use around 1730 and, although it is heresy to say so, may have been invented by an Englishman. A solemn, mostly spurious convention exists as to who is entitled to wear which tartan. There are no real evidence that early tartans were regarded as the inalienable property of individual clans, though it seems likely that over the years the most popular sett or pattern worn in a given locality would have been appropriated by the dominant clan. One of the few tartans that shows any consistency between past and present, I'm unreasonably proud to say, is the green, black, and white of the Macleans, first described in 1587. While a tribute to the skills of the local weaver, I would hesitate to suggest that the Maclean or any other "ancient" tartan had a particular tribal significance. The idea that Highland chiefs used tartan as a military uniform by which one clan could be distinguished from another is equally fanciful. On the battlefield, the belted plaid was commonly laid aside before a fight to allow greater freedom of action. Nor did tartans serve as camouflage. It has been said that a man only had to wrap himself in his plaid and lie down in his native heather to become invisible. The evidence suggests rather that the Highlander delighted in bright colors and, when he could afford it, elaborate finery. Even today, there can be few more resplendent sights than a Highland chief in full array. Ironically, the first tartan that could boast a name and corporate identity was the Black Watch, which was devised specifically to be worn by regiments raised for King George (largely recruited from Whig or Hanoverian clans) to police the Highlands after the Jacobite Rising of 1715. The somber green and black checkered pattern has been enormously influential ever since, not just in military fashions, but around the world in the designs of everything from luggage to boxer shorts. Once a symbol of suppression, it has become the one tartan that everyone feels comfortably entitled to wear. **U**ntil the eighteenth century, outside the Highlands the wearing of tartan carried the stigma of brigandry, primitiveness, and poverty. The attitude of condescension toward the Highlander, commonly regarded as little better than a savage, is caught by the Lowland laird, who, on being asked if his family had its own tartan, replied stiffly: "No, thank God. My ancestors were always able to afford trousers." In 1707, however, the unpopular Act of Union between Scotland and England had the effect of briefly uniting Scotland in its detestation of the English and founding a nationalist cause with which the wearing of tartan came to be enduringly associated. **A**fter the Jacobite defeat at Culloden in 1746, drastic steps were taken to pacify the Highlands and destroy the military power of the clans. In a direct assault on their pride, Highlanders were disarmed and prohibited by

Highland chief Sir Mungo Murray by Michael Wright, c. 1660, RIGHT, *an early example of the belted plaid. Piper to the Laird of Grant by Richard Waitt, 1714,* CENTER. *Not one of the four tartans worn by the Macdonald children,* FAR RIGHT, *in an eighteenth-century portrait by Jeremiah Davison, bears any resemblance to the modern Macdonald tartan.* Scottish National Portrait Gallery *(right and far right). Tartans,* LEFT TO RIGHT, *are the Muted Hunting Macintosh, the Muted Red Fraser, and the Red/Green Erskine.*

law from wearing tartan—the "garb of sedition." Failure to comply could get a man transported to the colonies. Enforced more or less brutally for thirty-five years, the Dress Act had the unintended effect, like any prohibition, of glamorizing the outlawed article. Nonetheless, by the time the law was repealed in 1783, it had helped achieve its avowed aim of breaking down the cohesive structure of Highland life. It wasn't until long after the Forty-Five, when the story of the rebellion had taken on the distant gleam of legend, that tartan really began to have a universal appeal. In the same paradoxical way that Native Americans only became the object of legitimate concern once their culture had been destroyed, so did the Highlands during the age of gradual decay that followed the destruction of the clan system enjoy an extraordinary revival of interest. Sir Walter Scott has often been held responsible for the re-tartanization of Scotland. His romantic Waverley novels certainly inspired the fashion for all things Highland that reached its puffing climax with King George IV's 1822 state visit to Edinburgh, where, draped in Royal Stewart tartan, the king enthusiastically proposed a toast of "Health to the Chieftans and Clans." The rage for tartan occasioned by the king's visit started a boom in manufacturing, influenced Paris style, and created a brisk demand for clan patterns as "gentlemen's fall wear" as

far away as New York. Tartan has never really been out of fashion since. But it was the Victorians who took the Celtic revival to absurd limits, reveling in an orgy of improving sentiment and arcane tartan scholarship. John and Charles Sobieski Stuart, an eccentric pair of impostors who claimed to be the legitimate grandsons of Prince Charles Edward, wrote best-selling books about Highland dress (based on research as dubious as their own origins), yet were inspired by a delusional sincerity typical of the age. Efforts to distinguish and catalog the "genuine" clan tartans were soon overwhelmed by the proliferation of new setts invented by shrewd weavers and tartan manufacturers. The example set by Queen Victoria, who first visited Scotland in 1842 and ten years later was carpeting and curtaining Balmoral Castle in acres of Royal Stewart, legitimized the tartan motif as a decorating notion, inevitably leading to excesses in the uses to which tartans were put. Today, every tourist shop in the country carries the tawdry souvenirs not of Scotland, but of the nineteenth century's passionate romance with the Highlands. It should not be forgotten, however, that it was the Scots themselves who led the way then as now in tartan-mania, supporting the fashion that has given them a wearable identity, a welcome excuse for dressing up, and a continuing link with the heroic myths of the past.

The days' doings in the Summer at Morar did not vary much; in general they were as follows: the children, governess, and nurse started as soon as lessons were over, or earlier if it was holiday time, for the sea. They embarked first of all in a boat on the loch at the foot of the house, and then changed into another —a sea boat below the bridge over the River Morar, to get to a bathing place.

Morar's silver sands have been celebrated in poetry and song. Blessed tranquillity and the ever-changing light give the beach at Camusdarrach, RIGHT, its magical quality. LEFT, Morar Lodge.

MORAR

IN 1881, WHEN MY GREAT-GRAND-
mother, Alice, Lady Lovat, wrote these lines, the
lodge at Morar had only just been built, but the
rhythms of life there had already been established and, with small variations, they have
scarcely changed since. A holiday home, rather
than strictly a shooting or fishing lodge (though
the Morar was known as one of the best sea trout
rivers in Scotland), Morar has always been associated in my family with children, with the sea-
side, and with a free (or minimally supervised)
existence that successive generations have
looked back on as the unbroken idyll of Highland childhood.

The bathing place that we favored when I was
growing up in the 1950s was the beach at Camusdarrach. A virginal stretch of silver-white sand
hidden by high cliff-like dunes from the single-
track Arisaig to Mallaig road, it looks out across
the Sea of the Hebrides to the exotic-sounding
(at least to non-Gaelic ears) islands of Eigg,
Rum, and Muck. At dusk, I remember, the setting sun seemed to turn their distinctive profiles
into one long silhouette as darkly inviting as the
coast of Africa. Even on a dull day, the beach
had a radiant tranquillity that I now ascribe to
the soft, sea-reflected, western light but believed
then to be proof of its enchantment. Although
more people have come to discover and enjoy
Camusdarrach, none of its magical qualities
have been lost nor has its memory been dimin-
ished by time. I can still find the places where,
as children, we used to spend hours poring over
rock pools, hunting for cowrie shells, or making

With its lush garden running down to the shores of Loch Morar, RIGHT, *secluded Morar Lodge,* BELOW, *looks out over the wooded islands, where the original forest that once covered most of the Highlands survives intact. The south-facing veranda is garlanded with clematis. A gravel path leads past the house down to the neatly kept vegetable garden.*

The inimitable drawing room at Morar, LEFT *and* ABOVE, *where the traditional woodlined walls and ceiling once painted white have mellowed to the color of smoke, inspiring David Scott's sketch,* TOP.

toboggan runs down the spike-grassed dunes under which we would sit in tribal groups and eat gritty picnics in all weathers. An extended family of cousins, we came to Morar most summers and stayed for a week or two not at the Lodge, where my grandfather's widowed sister, Aunt Peggy, lived and carried on the Lovat tradition of service to the community, but squashed into rented rooms in a nearby farmhouse that smelled of sea kale and porridge, and which we preferred because there was no need to be on our best behavior, and it was nearer the beach.

There were occasions, of course, when we would be invited up to the Lodge, but, a mile or more from the sea, it seemed a world apart. While over the years I got to know and love the house, with its long, yet intimate, wood-lined drawing room, its enormous Edwardian bathtubs ensconced in tiny, rather Spartan bathrooms, and its snug, gossipy, engine-room of a kitchen, I only learned to appreciate its charm

and its influence as a model for the way all houses should feel by a kind of osmosis. What interested me more as a boy were the legends about Morar I heard from Annie Macdonald, who ruled over the Gaelic-speaking kitchen at the Lodge, but often treated us children to tea and stories in her cottage at Camusdarrach. I remember being spellbound by her matter-of-fact description of Mhorag, the Loch Morar monster, a creature with as fair a claim as the swimmer in Loch Ness to scientific credibility.

Another yarn Annie spun between forays into local gossip came under the scarcely differentiated category of history. Her account of my ancestor Simon Lovat's capture by the English redcoats on Loch Morar after the Forty-Five made it seem as if the events happened only yesterday. It was on Eilean Ban, one of the wooded islands at the western end of the loch, that a secret seminary was founded in 1713 by the first bishop of the Highlands. At the time, Morar was the center of Catholicism in the Highlands, where, after the Reformation had brought Protestantism to Scotland, the old faith owed its survival to the devoutness of people in the remote glens (rather than, as in England, to a few powerful recusant families). After Culloden, when the English were searching the west coast for Bonnie Prince Charlie and his rebel supporters, putting the countryside to fire and sword as they went, old Lord Lovat (who had chosen the wrong moment to change sides) was given refuge on Eilean Ban by Bishop Hugh Macdonald, who like most Highland Catholics

The sideboard in the dining room, OPPOSITE BOTTOM, *under a collection of Nicholson woodcuts and shelves of books.* BELOW, *St. George grapples with a dragon on the stairway.*

The kitchen at Morar has always been the heart of the house, OVERLEAF. *In Annie Macdonald's day, the sound of Gaelic conversation rose to the bedrooms above,* OPPOSITE TOP, *which, without being luxurious, provide all the necessary comforts.*

was a staunch Jacobite. As a precaution, they brought all the boats on Loch Morar over to the island, but failed to reckon on the English carrying their own boats up the river from the sea. The Jacobites fled for their lives and, while Bishop Macdonald eventually escaped to France, the eighty-year-old Lovat, who begged to be left to his fate, was found hiding in a hollow tree. Captured and taken to London, he enjoyed the distinction of being the last peer of the realm to be beheaded—a sentence he met with great courage and dignity.

From the bedroom windows at Morar Lodge, Eilean Ban forms part of the view that by romantic association as much as physical beauty persuaded my great-grandmother to site the house there. Some years later, two of her sons were almost drowned in a boating incident close by and, out of gratitude, as a way of commemorating the narrowly averted tragedy, she helped the parish put up a cross on the hill and, later, build a new Catholic church on the shores of the loch. When I was a child, the tribes of cousins were taken to Mass there every Sunday under protest, dragged sandy-heeled from the magical beach. Now, I do the same with my own children. My cousin, Irene Stirling, who lived at Morar Lodge until this year, carried on its tradition of Highland hospitality toward succeeding generations as well as playing her part, unforgettably, in the life of the Morar community. And so the stories and legends about Morar, past and present, get handed on, connect, and become part of the life of the house.

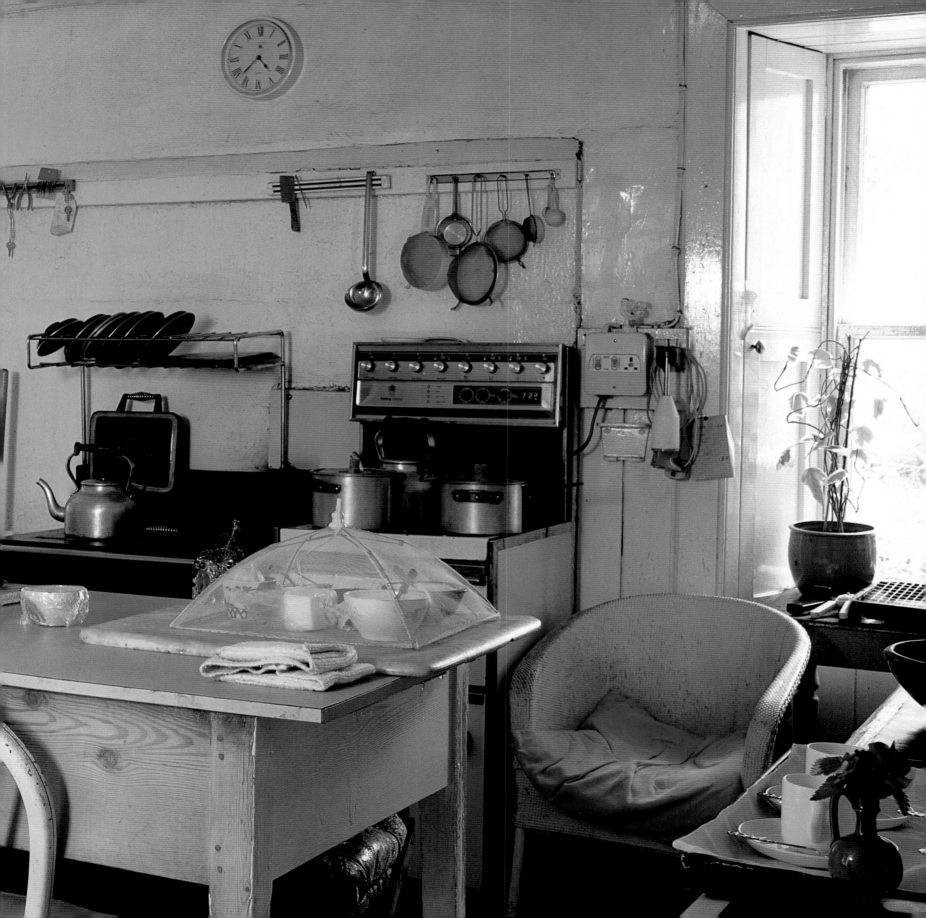

A GLANCE AT THE MAP SHOWS HOW DIFFI-cult it is to travel any distance in Scotland without coming across water. The coast is heavily indented with sea-lochs that run deep into the hills, so that you are never more than sixty miles from the sea. Inland, a multitude of rivers and lochs—nine thousand distinct bodies of freshwater—gives an often bleak landscape the picturesque impression of being filigreed with silver, promising untold rewards for fishermen. Early travelers in Scotland were astonished by the abundance of fish, particularly salmon and brown trout, inhabiting these rocky, fast-flowing rivers and cold, peaty lochs. The River Beauly was formerly so prolific of salmon, one observer relates, that a Lovat chief who lit a fire under a cauldron he had set beside the Beauly Falls only had to wait a minute or two before a salmon obliged him by leaping out of the river and into the pot, where it was soon cooked. The fish have become wiser, though fewer, since then, but even today, when salmon are being netted at sea and farmed in cages around the coast, considerable numbers are still caught on a rod every year for sport. There are some two hundred prime salmon streams in Scotland, providing fishing of an unusually varied range. A great river like the Tweed, broad, slow-moving, and mostly fished from a boat, cannot be compared to one of the small spate rivers, say the Borgie, in the far north. It seems barely conceivable that the same species run in both. Yet,

RIVER AND LOCH

A Lorne fisherman, OPPOSITE, *descends on a remote hill loch for an afternoon's sport, confident of bringing home a creelful of brown trout.*

the two rivers are, in their different ways, equally exciting to fish. The larger flow tends to attract larger salmon, but the size of the fish—as the true angler will tell you—is incidental to one's enjoyment of the sport. Nonetheless, a store of legend, the blindness of luck, and eternal optimism fuels the pursuit of the monster salmon. I remember being hopelessly influenced as a child by the story of the French chef at Beaufort, a M. Darde, who caused consternation by disappearing on the day of an important lunch party. The chef, who had never fished before in his life, had last been seen after breakfast trying his luck on the river. He was found by my grandfather at Grome Pool, still playing the salmon he'd hooked three hours earlier on a worm and a bent pin. Lunch was forgotten while my grandfather, acting as the chef's gillie, talked the exhausted M. Darde through the final stages of landing a salmon that would tip the scales at forty-seven pounds, the unbroken record for the largest fish taken from the Beauly. The challenge of fishing a big river like the Tweed or the Beauly is that it stretches your casting ability to its limits, and beyond. Nobody fishing today with conventional fishing tackle can achieve the distances that the legendary Archie Grant used to cast on the Spey in the 1930s. Using a twenty-two-foot rod from a boat he could cover sixty-five yards without shooting any line at all, lifting the whole length off the water. The lightness of modern graphite equipment has made casting easier, but it cannot compete with an old two-handed greenheart or split-cane salmon rod wielded by an expert. At the other extreme, stalking a fish on a small spate river, standing ten or fifteen feet back from the bank for fear of being seen and casting very gently with most of your line landing on dry ground, can be an absorbing pastime. In either case, while it may be satisfying to exercise a skill, the aim is to catch fish. Few fishermen enjoy flogging dead water. There is an intellectual dimension to fishing, some believe, which comes down to knowing when not to fish. But, having made an expensive commitment (the top salmon beats can cost $2,000 a day), most of us will choose to persevere. No one, after all, can be one hundred percent sure the next cast won't bring a strike. When the salmon aren't taking, on many rivers and lochs the prospect of catching sea trout is no less beguiling. A silvered, migratory form of brown trout that fight harder and, some say, have a more delicate flavor than salmon, sea trout are mostly caught at night, when fishing for them becomes a sport in its own right. Although sea trout run quite big (up to seven or eight pounds) in northern lochs or a river like the Spey, the difficulties of fishing blind, ideally on a night with no moon, favor using light

OPPOSITE, *success on a salmon river is less predictable. When conditions are unfavorable, choosing the right fly and knowing where to cast it can make all the difference, but few fishermen would deny the importance of luck.*

tackle. On alert, all your senses straining into the darkness, there is little to beat the thrill of an unseen quarry taking your fly with a surge sudden and strong enough to strip a reel or break a rod. It's the unexpected that makes fishing so engrossing, and at times frustrating, as a sport. A slow, mostly solitary activity, it demands close involvement with the river and surrounding countryside, which in Scotland can become part of the obsession. On a secluded pool, you may be lucky enough to see otters, herons, or ospreys engaged in the same activity as you—fishing. It will hardly make up for not catching anything, but it's an added delight that most sportsmen would not otherwise have the opportunity or the patience to discover. For more dependable results, fishing for brown trout in hill lochs offers an enjoyable day (with family, friends, dogs, and a picnic in tow) that rarely fails to yield a catch. Widely available, permits for trout fishing are not expensive. Even salmon fishing on Scotland's small rivers can seem surprisingly affordable when compared to what it costs in other countries. More and bigger fish may be taken in Alaska or Iceland, but the sporting tradition, the beauty of the land, and the huge variety of silver water support Scotland's claim to the best fishing in the world.

On the shores of Loch Fyne, Strachur House, LEFT, was built in 1783 by General John Campbell, a commander of the British forces in the Revolutionary War. The kitchen at Strachur, RIGHT, where fresh produce still comes from the home farm and garden.

STRACHUR

IN THE EARLY 1780S, GENERAL JOHN
Campbell, a commander of the British forces in
the American War of Independence, returned
to Scotland weary of battles and crowned with
sufficient glory to want to settle down to a quiet
life in his native Argyll. As a distinguished sol-
dier and chief of Clan MacArthur, General
Campbell decided to build himself a suitably imposing new house at Strachur on the shores of
Loch Fyne, where his ancestors had lived since
the days of the broch people. A plain classical
country seat of the type Highland lairds began
to construct in the latter, more prosperous half
of the eighteenth century, Strachur Park, as the
general proudly called it, represented a significant departure from the old huddle of a family
home he had abandoned back in the hills.
Around the new house, "pitched on a large
plain," Campbell laid out a two-acre garden and
a park, which was an English concept quite foreign to the Highlands, with beech avenues and
stands of silver and Scots firs planted, according
to his descendants, in the formation of one of

In the book-filled study,
RIGHT, *a massive
partners' Sheraton desk
looks out to three hills
behind the house that
correspond with the three
full-height bay windows.
The flagstoned hall,*
BELOW LEFT, *may
originally have been two
or more rooms.*

his more successful American engagements.

"Strachur Park is a very great ornament to this part of the Highlands," wrote the Reverend Charles Stewart, the local minister, in his 1792 account of the district. "It appears to the greatest advantage, viewed from the road that is carried down the opposite shore of Loch Fyne. A large basin, which is formed by a curve of the loch, lies immediately before the principal front of the house. The other front commands a view of the whole pleasure grounds, and of the neighbouring hills . . . Everything about it has a new, neat, and finished look."

The views from the house, framed by the now-massive beeches that General Campbell planted two hundred years ago, are otherwise unchanged. The nearby estate and farm buildings, reached by an ornate eighteenth-century bridge over the burn that runs through the garden, no longer look new, but still give an impression of well-favored orderliness that complements the simple elegance of the house.

The oval bedroom with its canopied bed, ABOVE, *overlooks the garden and has a more Victorian feel than the rest of the house.*

There is no record of whether an architect was involved in the building of Strachur. More than likely General Campbell designed the house himself with the help of a local master-builder, though his kinship with the Duke of Argyll may have enabled him to lean on the advice of Robert Adam, the celebrated Scottish architect, who at the time was involved in restoration work across the loch at Inveraray Castle. While no attempt was made to match Inveraray's extraordinary Gothic Revival architecture—or the

"total defiance of expense," which Dr. Johnson admired as contributing to the "grandeur and elegance of this Princely seat"—the two houses share some interior features, including Adam chimney pieces, a number of classical moldings, and a stone central staircase of cantilever construction, gracefully supported by its own weight.

Unfortunately, General Campbell died without leaving an heir and Strachur Park passed to his niece, who was either disinclined or unable

In the rainy West Highlands, the drying room, LEFT, where wet clothes and laundry are dried and aired and logs, coats, and boots are stored, is an essential part of country life.

RIGHT, *though worn and chipped, the old sinks with brass faucets in the scullery are valued for their enormous capacity. The wooden plate rack is indispensable.*

The stone cantilever staircase, supported by its own weight, ABOVE, *is similar to one at Inveraray Castle across Loch Fyne. The landing leads to the drawing room,* RIGHT, *and a king-size bathroom,* OPPOSITE.

to afford its upkeep. For many years the estate was let to an Edinburgh Law Lord, Lord Murray, and his cultivated, musical wife, who as a former pupil of Chopin felt herself to be a cut or two above her wild, moss-backed Argyllshire neighbors. In September 1848, while touring Scotland to raise money for his beloved Poland, Chopin sailed across the Clyde from Glasgow to spend a week at Strachur as Lady Murray's guest. Despite her efforts to make the ailing composer's stay a success, Chopin found Stra-

chur no more congenial than the rest of the Highlands. His bad health affected his playing; he disliked being stared at by the locals as though he were some exotic freak in a traveling circus; and he complained constantly of the cold, the damp, and the hideous discomfort. In what is now known as the far drawing room, Chopin gave a recital for Lady Murray's more refined friends. A handsomely proportioned room with a lofty ceiling, fine parquet floor, and mahogany doors, it not only has a light and gracious ambience, but excellent acoustics.

The house changed hands several times during the nineteenth and first half of the twentieth century. The present owners have lived there thirty-five years, yet Strachur has that indefinable atmosphere of a house inhabited by the same family for generations. Over the years a number of additions were made, the least congruous being the 1920s front porch and a service wing. But the eighteenth-century inscape of the building—its generous, life-embracing spirit—has hardly been affected. On the *piano nobile* (often above ground level in Scottish houses), the

194

house is only one room wide so that even on an overcast day the interior is never gloomy. Tall Venetian windows illuminate the open staircase and its spacious landings, presiding over a view of sea, sky, and hills that seems to flood the house with the soft, refracted light of the West.

A revelational advance on the narrow windows, hunched walls, and dark, twisting stairs of the old Scots Baronial architecture, the openness of Strachur inevitably suggests an affinity, even in the wilds of Argyll, with a new sensibility and enlightenment. The result may seem rough and ready when compared to the more elaborate design and finer quality of similar houses in the South. Something in the Scots character tends to shun conspicuous extravagance, equating plain living with elevated thoughts, adornment with damnation. The fact that many small Scottish landowners, like General Campbell, approved the ideals but could not afford the embellishments of classical architecture resulted in a type of Georgian country house that was distinctly Scottish in its ability to turn thrift and necessity to elegant advantage.

L O C

In the northern Highlands, the baronialized stalking lodge of Lochluichart, LEFT, epitomizes the golden age of the Victorian sporting life. RIGHT, looking out across Loch Luichart to the 40,000-acre deer forest.

HLUICHART

AS DEERSTALKING BECAME THE FASHION in Scotland, well-to-do Victorians (following the prince consort's example) rushed to buy or build a stalking lodge on a few thousand acres of Highland heath, where for three months of the year they had to pretend they were enjoying themselves. The "Scottish season," as it came to be known, gave lodge life (plainly Germanic in its romanticization of blood-letting in the wild) the ritual form it retains today as an exclusive, socially acceptable way of experiencing the Highland scene. Remote by definition, Victorian stalking lodges catered essentially to "men only" camping holidays, their spartan, wood-lined in-teriors more reminiscent of a Bavarian *Jägerhütte* than the ancient hunting tower or simple High-land bothy they replaced. While many of these traditionally male preserves have been either modernized or converted into family homes, Lochluichart Lodge in far Ross-shire enjoys the heretical distinction of having originally been designed for the comfort—that is, the Victorian idea of comfort—of women.

A small, unashamedly pretty house of pink granite trimmed with blue-gray slate and paint-work, it stands high above Loch Luichart with commanding views over the estate's forty-thousand acres of deer forest. Bought by Lord

Ashburton in the 1850s, the lodge owed its "feminine" character to his widow, Louisa, who had grown up at nearby Brahan Castle and who, after her husband's death in 1864, made Lochluichart her summer home. In the stalking season, she entertained there on a grand scale, filling the lodge (enlarged to sleep fourteen guests) and farming out any overspill to her mother at Brahan Castle. Influenced, like so many Highlanders, by the Victorian enthusiasm for the Scottish baronial style, Louisa later added on a tower and porch, threw out bay windows in the drawing room, and built a small village of outhouses that includes stables, a gunroom, fishing room, tackroom for the ponies, and rustic game larders with birch-log sides—all necessary to the smooth running of a Highland sporting establishment.

A Seaforth Mackenzie, descended from the ancient and ill-fated house of Kintail, Lady Ashburton was deeply rooted in Highland history. On the drawing-room mantelpiece at Lochluichart, there is a framed letter from Sir Walter Scott to Louisa's mother, who was known throughout Scotland as the "hooded lady" for the part she played in the famous prophesy of Kenneth Odhar, the "Brahan Seer": Condemned to death by the third Countess Seaforth for revealing her husband's infidelity, the Seer (a Highland Nostradamus) took his revenge at the stake by prophesying that the Mackenzie line would become extinct when a deaf and dumb chief survived his four sons and the heir to his

A hot bath after a hard day's stalking, one of life's great luxuries, can be enjoyed in this gigantic Edwardian tub encased in mahogany, OPPOSITE TOP. *The brass four-poster bed with chintz hangings in one of the bedrooms,* ABOVE, *looks no less inviting.* OPPOSITE BOTTOM, *the downstairs bathroom at Lochluichart.*

ruined estates—a white-hooded woman from the East—killed her own sister. The first part of the curse had already been fulfilled by the time Louisa's mother, now the new chief of Kintail, returned from India in 1815 wearing a white widow's cap. The last act of the tragedy unfolded in Louisa's lifetime when the hooded lady, driving her sister in a pony trap between Brahan Castle and Lochluichart, was involved in an accident which only she survived.

The prophecy had run its course, but Louisa, as proud of her Highland heritage as she was

There's no escaping the cult of the stag at Lochluichart:
Stags' heads bristle from the outhouses and gunroom,
ABOVE LEFT AND RIGHT, and the hall, LEFT. The
lodge walls are covered in paintings and drawings of stags,
which also fill the illustrated visitors' books and, in the case
of a Landseer collage, OPPOSITE BOTTOM LEFT, a
window in the dining room. The conservatory, OPPOSITE
TOP RIGHT, offers a peaceful haven in which to read a
book from the well-stocked sporting shelves.

Margaret Compton — Oct 9th 182. *So glad to come, so sorry to go!*

Northampton — no words to express my feelings on so ———

Mary Lowther   Oct 10th 1883.

My heart is as full at leaving, as this house generally is of guests!

Loch Na Fhea   Oct 8. 1883.   Rain.
"Lifeless, yet beautiful he lay."

superstitious, made the most of its romantic associations. A fey, artistic, yet forceful character, described as having "locomotive energy," she ran her stalking lodge as a Highland salon, surrounding herself with the well-known artists and writers she bagged on her travels. John Ruskin, Robert Browning, Millais, Sir Edwin Landseer, and Thomas Carlyle all stayed at Lochluichart. That they came for Lady Ashburton's company as much as for the stalking, can be inferred by their failure to keep the game larders well-supplied. Louisa once sent Carlyle a haunch of venison and complained, boasting a little, about the lack of grouse: "As my shooting lodge is filled with a succession of artists, musicians, literary men, and scientific savants, the game laughs at us and the forester is in despair."

Visitors stayed at least a week, often several. While the men were out stalking, the ladies would go for walks, read, and sketch. From game records and the remarkable illustrated visitors books at Lochluichart, one gets an idea of the innocent delight the Victorians took in the healthy pursuit of outdoor sports—the hairy-kneed romance of Highland life. One cannot help wondering how they coped with midges and the rain, but nothing seems to cloud the happy doggerel and idealized drawings they left beside their signatures. Some of the most amusing contributions are by Landseer, a close friend and old admirer of Louisa's. Much in demand socially, he would spend several weeks in the

A group of gillies and stalkers from Lochluichart's past, ABOVE, *sporting the traditional tweed cap, which is still an essential part of the hillman's gear, judging from the collection hanging on antlers in the front porch,* RIGHT.

Highlands every year, moving from one grand house to another. At Lochluichart, the walls are crowded with prints the artist sent to Louisa as thank-you notes. While staying there, one wet afternoon, Landseer made her a collage from brown wrapping and tissue paper that comes magically alive when held up to the light; the fragile image of stags getting wind of a stalking party remains suspended in the dining-room window, a reminder of how little has changed after more than a century.

On the tower, high above the porch, Louisa had enscribed the odd, admonitory couplet: "Watch and pray, Time hasteth away," as if she feared her beloved Lochluichart might share the ruinous fate of her accursed family. But the lodge has been handsomely refurbished by the present owners, who have managed to turn it into a family home and live there year-round without disturbing Louisa's ghost. Lady Eliza Leslie Melville, Louisa's great-granddaughter, has kept all the large furniture—the sofas, the leather armchairs, the pitch-pine wardrobes—as well as pictures, collected by Louisa or given to her, and shelves of Victorian novels and sporting books. Apart from dragging the plumbing into the twentieth century ("The only important thing about a stalking lodge," Eliza says firmly, "is to have enough hot water"), she takes pride in having successfully preserved the original character of the house, an unusual monument to the golden age of Victorian sporting life.

IT CAN COME AS A SHOCK TO DISCOVER that there are no mountains in Scotland. In local speech any rugged, treeless terrain, from the grouse moors of Perthshire to the ski slopes of Ben Aonach, is referred to simply as "the hill." Confronted by some soaring, snow-capped peak, the native observation, "A good day for the hill," may sound dauntingly wry; but with hill ground accounting for three-quarters of the country, the Scots have learned to make light of walking. Some of the most glorious sights in Scotland are guarded by distance, a forbidding remoteness that can only be challenged on foot. In *Kidnapped,* Robert Louis Stevenson's classic novel of the Highlands, the hero walks halfway across Scotland, taking to the hills at every opportunity. The novel's atavistic themes of survival and pursuit in the wild, drawn from Highland history—most notably, the fugitive Bonnie Prince Charlie's escape through the heather after Culloden—still have resonance today for every hiker who strides manfully off into the trackless distance followed by a cloud of midges. No wilderness in the world has been more thickly sown with romance, traces of which still flourish for some in those hill sports for which the Scottish countryside has long been famous: grouse shooting and deerstalking. **A**s one whose experience of the grouse moor is limited to the noncombatant driving of birds toward stationary guns, I have never looked forward to the "Glorious 12th" of August (when the grouse season

ON THE HILL

Scotland has vast areas of hill ground for those with the money and inclination to shoot grouse or stalk deer. The terrain can be extremely rugged and part of the enjoyment lies in the physical challenge of the wilderness. On a Perthshire grouse moor, OPPOSITE, a man welcomes the chance for a brief rest while the other guns catch up.

opens) with any great enthusiasm. An invariably damp, cleg-harried picnic—the idealized version has groaning hampers with white tablecloths spread out in the purple heather—seems to me a dubious high point to a testing day. But for the keen shot there is no doubt that dispatching grouse is one of the more difficult forms of game shooting. To stand on the flank of a steep moor trying to hit driven birds traveling at speeds of up to sixty miles an hour as they fly over a Maginot line of peat butts requires skill if not a great deal of energy. In Victorian times, the grouse on many estates were left to be shot by keepers at the end of the season. An activity that can now cost $4,000 a day to indulge was regarded then as not quite a gentleman's sport. **D**eerstalking in Scotland, on the other hand, has for centuries been considered the noblest of pastimes. On a well-run sporting estate, shooting deer is seen as part of an organized cull for the improvement of the herd. The young stags with the finest antlers are kept for breeding while the old, the sick, and the lame must be weeded out, leaving little opportunity for trophy hunting. Every spring, after their horns drop off (and are chewed up by the hinds to get the calcium they need for calving), the stags start growing new antlers, which remain soft and covered in velvet until about August. The season officially opens July 1, but seldom gets underway before the stags are out of velvet. One of the pleasures of stalking is that the skills employed allow you to observe animals behaving naturally in the wild. In the rut, or mating season, the spectacle of stags fighting over their hinds—one stag will hold a harem of some forty hinds—can distract the most dedicated hunter. The hinds, posted around the outside of the group, act as sentries so that the males can concentrate on bouts of ferocious combat, roaring, charging, boxing, and locking horns with each other in clashes that can be heard echoing through the hills for miles around. **A** typical day's stalking begins with a hearty Scotch breakfast, needed to fuel what can easily turn out to be a 25-mile hike. Usually, you go out alone with a stalker, or gillie, who (unless you are very experienced) is in charge at all times. The stalker decides when you walk, when you rest, when you crawl on all fours, when you stop to eat lunch—not a hamper and tablecloth affair, but the soggy sandwich, or "piece," you have been carrying in your pocket all day. He knows every inch of the hill, every gully and corrie and rocky outcrop. What he cannot know exactly is what you are going to see or be able to shoot, which ensures an element of surprise. **A** good stalker will often come from a long line of gillies and more than likely keep his eyes sharp by working as a shepherd out of season. Steeped in hill lore and craft, he can see if there is a shootable stag among a group of deer from what seems an impossible distance. He can tell the age and condition of every beast and will

Land Rovers, OPPOSITE TOP, *bring the guns to within striking distance of the moor and may save carrying the lunch hampers. In contrast to the grouse-shooting picnic,* OPPOSITE BOTTOM, *a leisurely affair (weather permitting), the deer stalker often has to make do with a single hasty sandwich.*

only let you shoot the one that needs to be shot. Once he has chosen your quarry, he will bring you close enough to that stag for a clean kill, even if it takes all day. Unless, of course, something untoward happens. The wind may change: in a corrie, it can swirl round and catch you on the back of the neck; or, you may come creeping over the brow of a hill, having made a lengthy detour in order to stay downwind of a herd, only to find the glen maddeningly empty, the deer vanished. **T**he physical challenge of stalking, walking for miles over steep, rugged terrain, working the wind, crawling on one's belly through bogs and up icy burns, makes this a sport where, for enjoyment's sake, the stalk itself must be at least as important as the kill. Of all blood sports, stalking demands the closest involvement with the natural world, particularly the land. The feeling of kinship with the wilderness can produce moments of sheer exhilaration that compound the thrill of the chase. One works extraordinarily hard for a single shot, knowing that the stag has at least a twenty-to-one chance of getting away. After a long, grueling stalk, the inadmissible voice inside pleads: Anything to be able to go home. Of course, every hunter would rather experience the cathartic release of dispatching his prey, but there is always the promise of a glass or two of whisky and a long, hot bath at the end of a kill-less but rewarding day.

A R D

Highland cattle graze in "the park," RIGHT, as the field in front of Ardkinglas is known. A neobaronial mansion, Ardkinglas was built by Edwardian architect Robert Lorimer as a shooting lodge for Sir Andrew Noble. His great-grandson, Johnny Noble, LEFT, stands on the S-shaped exterior staircase that leads from a hidden door in the paneled drawing room.

KINGLAS

The latest in Edwardian weather monitoring equipment, used to help sportsmen plan their days on the hill, still warns of approaching storms. The pillared upper hall, ABOVE LEFT AND RIGHT, *gives onto a loggia overlooking Loch Fyne.* ABOVE CENTER, *hats for all weathers under a parliament clock in the lower hall.*

ground up for a client, a "new man" preferably, to whom expense would be no object.

Sir Andrew Noble, who commissioned Ardkinglas, was precisely such a man. An expatriate Scot, who had made his fortune as chairman of Armstrong, the Tyneside armaments firm, he wanted to build a suitably impressive mansion on his vast Argyllshire estates chiefly to please his Scots-Canadian wife, who had always longed to return to Noble territory on the west coast of Scotland. The Nobles gave Lorimer a remarkably free hand, inviting him to design, build, and furbish the entire house down to the last detail. Sir Andrew's forceful daughter, Lilias, liaised with the architect and his craftsmen, but her instructions were simple: Nothing but the best, hang the expense—and get on with it. The

patriarchal Sir Andrew, by then well into his seventies, was in something of a hurry.

Ardkinglas was finished in an astonishing eighteen months at a cost of £55,000 (roughly $5 million today)—a not inconsiderable sum to spend on a holiday home. But Sir Andrew was an extravagant tycoon; far from the popular image of the penny-pinching Scots businessman, he liked to entertain on a lavish scale. The endless house parties that shot and fished and worked up appetites on the hill for gargantuan meals had to be accommodated in comfort and style. Lorimer interpreted his client's Edwardian exuberance in his designs for a Highland pleasure-drome that nonetheless showed an inspired appreciation for their country's architectural heritage.

A child's rocking horse, ABOVE RIGHT, *finds a niche in one of the fireplaces lined with antique Dutch tiles in the billiard room. Ardkinglas is full of corners where one can sit quietly,* ABOVE LEFT, *and perhaps read a book or enjoy a view.*

Although his more famous contemporary, Charles Rennie Mackintosh, came nearer to transforming Scottish vernacular architecture with a genuinely modern vision, Sir Robert Lorimer was the first to discover and assimilate a living architectural tradition in Scotland. After his death, the geographical isolation of much of Lorimer's work, its rareness—Ardkinglas is one of only four houses he designed himself—and the reaction against Romanticism in architecture contributed to the decline of a reputation that has only lately begun to be restored. Lorimer never abandoned his traditional ideals and Ardkinglas, the last great country house to be built in Scotland, may be seen as the swan song of baronial invention.

In search of a more contemporary style, Lori-

In the drawing room, LEFT, life centers around the massive fireplace, which has a lintel carved from a single block of granite weighing five tons. A framed reminder of meal and post times, BELOW, recalls the days when Ardkinglas was run like a hotel for nonpaying friends and relations. ABOVE, the dining room has wonderful views of the garden.

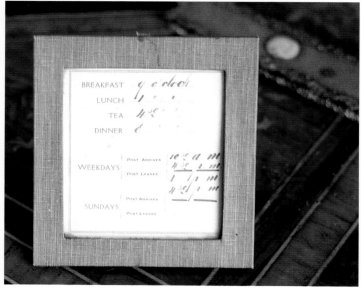

mer brought to the traditionally austere lines of Ardkinglas with its corbelled turrets, stepped gables, and breakneck roofs the gentling influence of luxury, light, and an easeful sense of grace. It tells in the rich accumulation of detail: from the decorated plaster ceilings, the curving exterior staircases, the raised dais in the billiards room where spectators could lounge with a fire at their backs, to the original designs for the light fixtures, fireplaces, door handles, and even keyhole flaps. Influenced by Art Nouveau and the Scottish Arts and Crafts movement, Lorimer and his Edinburgh craftsmen used the artistic freedom given them by Sir Andrew's new money to produce a house remarkable in its decorative detail, modern in the practical aspects of its design, and, above all, comfortable.

It was inevitable that following generations of Nobles would choose to make Ardkinglas a permanent home. Sir Andrew died in 1915, "called

The morning room, TOP LEFT, *looks out to the oyster beds on the shores of Loch Fyne. The Anastasia room,* TOP RIGHT, *like most of the bedrooms at Ardkinglas,* RIGHT, *has a fine plasterwork ceiling decorated by Edinburgh craftsmen. The vine motif is based on a traditional pattern. An extra-deep tub,* ABOVE.

over," a romantic account has it, by the roaring of stags in Glen Kinglas as the reluctant laird breathed his last. The blithe age of Edwardian summering in Scotland had come to an end, and after the intervention of two world wars, life at Ardkinglas would never be the same.

Johnny Noble, Sir Andrew's great-grandson, who grew up at Ardkinglas, remembers roaming around the neglected policies in a gang of half-wild children: "For a boy keen on outdoor pursuits, it would be hard to imagine a more enthralling childhood world." When he inherited the estate from his father in 1972 and returned to live there, circumstances were less encouraging. He could still afford to enjoy its Buchanesque pleasures and to entertain, if not as lavishly as the Edwardians, then generously enough to fill the great house with seasonal spates of family and friends. But like many a Highland laird, he had to find new ways of

The tiled kitchen and scullery, ABOVE and ABOVE RIGHT, where a large staff once catered for a never-ending house party, are still used and provide the luxury of space.

DAIRY WASHING

The labeled storerooms along the kitchen passage, LEFT, were essential to running a self-sufficient household. Hand basins and pitchers in bedroom alcoves, FAR LEFT and RIGHT.

CAKES & CONFECTIONERY

KITCHEN STORES

BREAD

CREAM

adapting a traditionally unhurried, uncommercial life to the present day. At Ardkinglas, this meant turning the estate, which was created for a rich man's entertainment, into a center of local industry.

Johnny still employs people from the nearby village of Cairndow whose fathers had worked for his father, but the estate has become leaner, more diversified. "The days of seven gardeners toiling away to produce vegetables for the 'big house' are long gone," he says without regret. "Whether the sheep lived or died didn't make a ha'p'worth of difference to my great-grandfather. To me it does. But if you include all the tenanted enterprises being run from the estate, Ardkinglas provides as many if not more jobs than it did in Andrew Noble's time."

Ten years ago, looking for ways to meet the growing costs of keeping up the house, Johnny started to grow oysters from seed on the shores of Loch Fyne. The project soon developed into a thriving seafood concern that now sends out

The stylish light fixtures, ABOVE *and* OPPOSITE, *were all designed by Lorimer. One of the first country houses to have electricity, Ardkinglas could boast its own power station: The chandeliers proudly display bare bulbs.* ABOVE RIGHT, *the pride and joy of Ardkinglas plumbing, this unusual shower is an example of Lorimer's obsession with modernity.*

fresh oysters, langoustines, smoked salmon, and kippers all over the world. At low tide, you can see the oyster beds from the morning-room windows. In the middle of the loch, a flotilla of salmon cages leased by the estate to a fish-farming tenant has also become part of the view. Sir Andrew may be turning in his grave, but Johnny insists he has learned to love the cages. Certainly Lorimer, who believed in exploiting the natural resources of a locality, would have approved of Johnny's pragmatic, relaxed attitude toward life at Ardkinglas.

He lives in solitary splendor, very much the Highland gentleman, though a habit of wearing frayed fisherman's smocks over ancient tweed or tartan breeks makes it easy to mistake the laird for one of those toiling gardeners out of the Edwardian past. Although it can be a little bleak in winter, Johnny claims that Ardkinglas is an easy and comfortably compact house to run. Inured to most of its inconveniences, he's never found rattling around his baronial fastness a

A pear tree grows on the west side of the house, ABOVE. *Picking daffodils in the half-wild garden near the old tennis court,* RIGHT.

hardship; not when weighed against the inestimable luxuries of self-sufficiency. "It may seem eccentric to some people," the laird of Ardkinglas concedes, "my living here as I do, but how many places can you go out and catch a salmon, or shoot a woodcock for dinner, or walk down to the shore and gather your own oysters?"

When he's forced to talk about the success of his own efforts to turn the estate to commercial account, what comes across more strongly than Johnny Noble's sense of achievement is his abiding love of the place. On a balmy June evening, looking down Loch Fyne from the sun-drenched loggia, one can understand—at least until the midges come out—why the spell cast by Lorimer, in what he considered the perfect setting for a Scottish country house, has never been broken.

A rare view of Ardkinglas from the water, RIGHT. The date construction of the house was completed—in an astonishing eighteen months—was carved over the front door, ABOVE RIGHT. Logs stacked inside the porch are cut to a generous length for the great fireplace in the drawing room, BELOW RIGHT. The ornately carved leg of a fold-down table on the loggia, BELOW LEFT, is typical of Lorimer's extraordinary attention to detail. ABOVE LEFT, Johnny Noble and Andy Lane, his partner in the seafood business, working on the oyster beds.

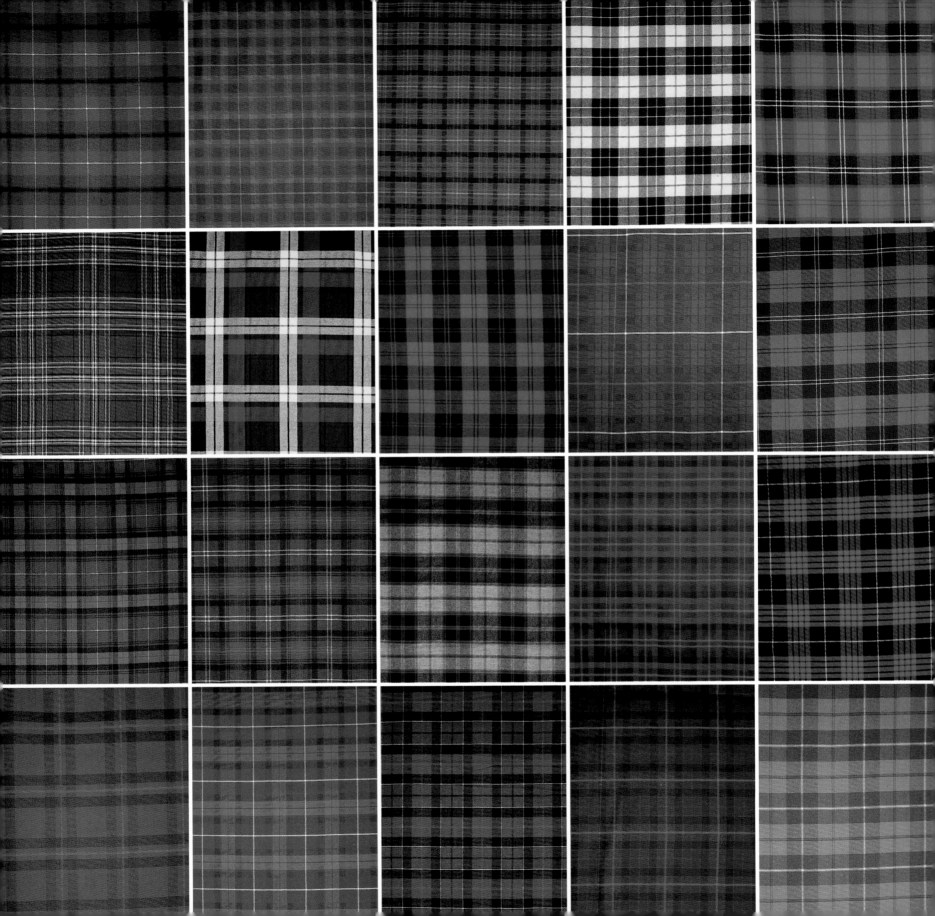

TOP ROW: *Douglas (old colors), Muted Hunting Macintosh, Cameron of Erracht (old colors), Macleod Dress, Lennox.*
SECOND ROW: *Hunting MacFarlane (old colors), Macmillan Ancient, Red/Green Erskine, Hunting Fraser (old colors), Blue Ramsay.* THIRD ROW: *Ancient Hunting Lord of Thelsles, Ancient Sutherland (old colors), Hunting MacPherson, Hunting MacDuff, MacQueen.* BOTTOM ROW: *Elliot, Muted Red Fraser, Green Leslie (old colors), Gunn, Hunting Galloway.*

TIMELINE

A.D. 81–350	Romans establish outposts in Scotland
400	Saint Ninian, first Christian missionary, arrives
563	Saint Columba establishes Celtic church on Iona
844	Kenneth MacAlpin, King of the Scots, assimilates the Pictish tribes
1034	Scotland first united under Duncan I
1263	Norse control of the Hebrides ends with Battle of Largs
1297	William Wallace leads resistance movement for independence from England
1314	Robert the Bruce defeats English army at Bannockburn
1320	Declaration of Arbroath. Scotland's call to freedom
1371	Robert II (1371–90), first Stewart king
1414	St. Andrews University founded
1451	University of Glasgow founded
1503	James IV (1488–1513) marries Margaret Tudor, daughter of Henry VIII
1513	Battle of Flodden. The flower of Scots chivalry decimated by English army. James IV killed
1560	Reformation in Scotland led by John Knox
1587	Mary Queen of Scots executed
1603	Union of the Crowns under James VI of Scotland (I of England)

1638–1666	The National Covenant drafted. The Covenanters struggle to establish and defend Presbyterianism and prevent Scotland becoming a province of England
1689	First Jacobite Rebellion
1692	Massacre of Glencoe
1707	Union of Parliaments. Officially Scotland and England cease to exist as separate countries and become Great Britain
1715	Jacobite Rising. Highland clans rally for James Edward Stewart, in Jacobite eyes King James VIII of Scotland (III of England)
1730–1820	The Scottish Enlightenment
1745	The Forty-Five Rebellion. Prince Charles Edward raises the clans, wins several victories over Hanoverian forces, and marches on London
1746	Jacobites defeated at Battle of Culloden. Breakup of clan system
1750–1850	Highland Clearances
1759–1796	Robert Burns, Scotland's greatest lyric poet
1771–1832	Sir Walter Scott, Romantic novelist and poet
1822	George IV's state visit to Scotland

GLOSSARY

Architectural and Scottish Terms

ASTRAGAL. Window glazing bar

BARMEKIN. Defensive wall

BARTIZAN. Small projecting turret for sentry

BELL-CAST. Hipped (roof)

BLACK HOUSE. Windowless dwelling with thick rubble walls and thatched roof

BOTHY. A hill shelter

BREEKS. Trousers

BROCH. Iron Age circular tower

BURN. Small stream

BUT AND BEN. Two-roomed cottage

BYRE. Shelter for cows

CAPHOUSE. Top story (of tower) opening onto roof

CEILIDH. Informal gathering for singing, dancing, and storytelling

CLAYMORE. Two-edged broadsword used by Highlanders

CLEG. A horsefly

CORBEL. Projecting stone bracket

CORRIE. Circular hollow on a hillside

CREEL. Wickerwork basket used to hold fish or fishing tackle

CROFT. Small enclosed plot of land

CROTAL. Any of various lichens used for dyeing wool

CROW-STEPS. A set of steps on top of a gable

CURTAIN WALL. Outer defensive wall surrounding a castle enclosure

DOOCOT. Dovecote

DRYSTANE. (Of a wall) made without mortar

DUN. Small primitive fort usually built on a natural mound

GILLIE. A guide for hunting or fishing

GLEN. Narrow and deep valley

GUN LOOP. Small hole in fortified wall for use of firearms

HAG. Peat bog

HARLED. Covered with roughcast plaster

HOWE. Basin or valley

JACOBITE. Supporter of James II after his overthrow in 1688, or of his Stewart descendants

LAIRD. A landowner

MIDGE. Small mosquito-like biting insect

MULL. A promontory

NEOBARONIAL. Victorian revival of Scottish Baronial architectural style

PARTERRE. Formally patterned flower garden

PEEL TOWER. Medieval fortified tower

PHILABEG. Kilt

PIOBRAICH. Form of bagpipe music

PLAID. Long piece of cloth (usually tartan) worn over shoulder as part of Highland dress

POLICIES. Grounds surrounding a country house

SETT. Square in a tartan pattern or the pattern itself

SHIELING. Summer pasture for cattle

SHOTHOLE. See GUN LOOP

SKERRY. Small rocky island

STALKING. Deer hunting

STANDING STONE. Prehistoric megalith

STEADING. The outbuildings of a farm

TARGE. Shield

TURNPIKE OR WHEEL STAIR. Spiral staircase within a tower

WAULK. To make cloth heavier through shrinking and beating

DIRECTORY

Houses and Gardens Open to the Public

None of the principal houses featured in this book are open to the public. However, all the larger gardens and many of the better-known castles and houses mentioned in the text welcome visitors. The following list comprises some of outstanding interest.

Castles and Houses

ABBOTSFORD
Near Melrose
Roxburghshire
Open April to October
Phone (0896) 2043

BLAIR CASTLE
Blair Atholl
Perthshire
Open daily April 1 to
October 30
Phone 0796 481207

CASTLE FRASER
Near Kemnay
Aberdeenshire
Open May 1 to
September 30
Phone (033 03) 463

CAWDOR CASTLE
Inverness
Open May 1 to October 4
Phone 066 77 615

CRAIGIEVAR
Near Alford
Aberdeenshire
Open May 1 to
September 30
Phone (033 983) 635

CRATHES
Near Banchory
Kinkardineshire
Open May 1 to
September 30
Phone (033 044) 651

CULZEAN CASTLE
Near Maybole
Ayrshire
Open April to October
Phone (065 56) 274

DRUMLANRIG
Near Carronbridge
Dumfriesshire
Open May to August
Phone (0848) 30248 or
31682

DUNROBIN CASTLE
Golspie
Highlands
Open Monday to
Thursday in May; daily
June 1 to October 15
Phone 0408 633177/
268

GLAMIS CASTLE
Glamis
Perthshire
Open daily April 17 to
October 12
Phone 030784 242

HOPETOUN
Near Abercorn
West Lothian
Open April 17 to
October 4
Phone 031 331 2451

INVERARAY CASTLE
Near Inveraray
Argyllshire
Open April to October
Phone (0499) 2203

LENNOXLOVE
Haddington
Lothian
Open Wednesday,
Saturday, and Sunday;
May to September

MANDERSTON
Nr Duns
Berwickshire
Open Thursday and
Sunday May 14 to
April 27
Phone 0361 83450

MAXWELTON
Nr Thornhill
Dumfrieshire
Open Wednesday
through Sunday to end
of September
Phone 084 82 385

MELLERSTAIN
Nr Kelso
Berwickshire
Open daily (except
Saturday), May 1 to
September 30
Phone 057 381 225

TRAQUAIR
Nr Innerleithen
Berwickshire
Open Easter; Sunday
and Monday in May;
daily May 30 to
September 30
Phone 0896 830323

Gardens

ACHNACLOICH
Near Connel
Argyllshire
Open April 5 to
June 11

ARDUAINE
Near Loch Melfort
Argyllshire
Open April to
September

BRANKLYN GARDEN
Perth
Perthshire
Open daily March 1 to
October 30
Phone 0738 25535

CASTLE KENNEDY
GARDENS
Stranraer
Dumfrieshire
Open daily from Easter
through September

CRARAE
Near Minard
Argyllshire
Open all year

DRUMMOND CASTLE
Muthill
Tayside
Open daily May 1 to
August 31 from 2–6
P.M.; Wednesday and
Sunday only in
September

DUNDONNEL
Near Little Loch
Broom
Ross and Cromarty
Open only by special
appointment

GREENBANK
GARDEN
Glasgow
Open daily
Phone 042 639 3281

INVEREWE
Near Poolewe
Ross and Cromarty
Open all year
Phone (044 586) 200

KINROSS
Near Kinross
Kinrossshire
Open May to
September

LOGAN BOTANICAL
Near Port Logan
Wigtownshire
Open April to
September
Phone (077 686) 231

More details about visiting Scottish gardens can be had by contacting Scotland's Gardens Scheme, 31 Castle Terrace, Edinburgh EH4 3EU; phone 031 229 1870.

LADY LUCINDA
SHAW STEWART
Ardgowan
Inverkip
Renfrewshire
(0475 521) 226

LOVATT ANTIQUES
100 Torrisdale Street
Glasgow
041 423 6497

PERTH ANTIQUE
CENTRE
28 Glasgow Road
Perth
(0738 37) 473

Armor

THISTLE ARMS
Whitburn
West Lothian
(0501 43) 426

Art Galleries

BOURNE FINE ART
4 Dundas Street
Edinburgh
031 557 4050

THE FINE ART
SOCIETY
134 Blythswood Street
Glasgow
041 332 4027

THE SCOTTISH
GALLERY
94 George Street
Edinburgh
031 225 5955

THE WASHINGTON
GALLERY
44 Washington Street
Glasgow
041 221 6780

Fabrics and Wallpapers

ART FABRICS
146 West Regent Street
Glasgow
041 248 3322

THE FABRIC
WORKSHOP
5 Park Circus
Glasgow
041 332 6756

OSBORNE AND
LITTLE
39 Queen Street
Edinburgh
031 225 5068

Fireplaces

DUNEDIN ANTIQUES
6 North West Circus Place
Edinburgh
031 225 3074

STONECRAFT
FIREPLACES
Lower London Road
Edinburgh
031 652 1464

Pottery

THE ADAM
POTTERY
76 Henderson Row
Edinburgh
031 557 3978

Antiques and Things

There is no connection between the interior decoration of the houses featured in this book and the various firms mentioned below. But for anyone interested in Scottish collectibles or in re-creating Scottish style, the following list could be helpful as a starting point.

Antiques

ARCHITECTURAL
RECYCLING
COMPANY
Craighall
Rattray
Blairgowrie
(0250) 4749

CASTLE
RESTORATIONS
Auchtertool House
Auchtertool
Fife
(0592 780) 371

HAND IN HAND
3 North West Circus Place
Edinburgh
031 226 3598

Architects

Specialists in finding and restoring Scottish buildings from tower houses to Georgian mansions.

NICHOLAS
GROVES-RAINES AND
STEINHUS LTD.
Peffermill House
Peffermill Road
Edinburgh
031 661 7172

The Road to the Isles

Touring the Hebrides, it's as well to remember that travel arrangements are hostage to the weather, eccentric timetables, and a cultural prejudice against haste. "When God made time, He made plenty of it," goes an old Hebridean saying that catches the spirit of the Western Isles. It's all the advice anyone needs to enjoy this exceptionally beautiful and unspoiled part of the world.

The majority of inhabited islands can be reached with Caledonian Macbrayne, the steamer company that has been plying these waters for over a century. Inquiries to: Caledonian Macbrayne, The Ferry Terminal, Gourock; phone (0475) 33755.

If comfort comes before adventure, the cruiseship *Hebridean Princess* runs well-planned voyages with luxurious accommodation and gastronomic meals to help keep the scenery at a civilized remove. For reservations and information: Hebridean Island Cruises Ltd., Bank Newton, Skipton, Yorkshire; phone (0756) 748077.

Chartering a professionally skippered boat offers the best of all worlds—the freedom to cruise preferred islands in style and at one's own pace. Inquiries to:

BRUCE WATT
Mallaig Harbour
Invernessshire
Phone (0687) 2233

EDEN KENNEIL
Ardpatrick
Argyllshire
Phone (0880 820) 791

KYLEBAHN
CHARTERS LTD.
2 Church Road
Lyminge
Kent
Phone (0303 862) 727

MELFORT CHARTERS
Dunvegan House
Great Howard Street
Liverpool
Phone 051 207 4069

Where to Stay

Scotland is famous for the warmth of its hospitality and the friendliness of its people. Comfort and good food can be found in a growing number of excellent country hotels. The following are some of the less well-known but among the authors' personal favorites.

AIRDS HOTEL
Port Appin
Argyll
Phone 063173 236
High class small hotel with incredible views across Loch Linnhe. Wonderful food in Michelin-starred restaurant.

THE CREGGANS INN
Strachur
Argyllshire
Phone (036 986) 279
Character, comfort, and delicious food make this the ideal place from which to visit Scotland's west coast castles and gardens.

GREYWALLS
Muirfield, Gullane
East Lothian
Phone 0620 842144
Close to Edinburgh, this Lutyens house with its beautiful garden laid out by Gertrude Jekyll was once a favorite haunt of Edward VII. The proprietors, who are the third generation of the family to live here, make sure that it has the atmosphere of a well-loved country home.

ISLE OF ERISKA
Ledaig
Oban
Argyll
Phone 0631 72371
A totally secluded hotel situated on a three hundred-acre private island in the middle of Loch Linnhe. Delicious food and great comfort.

KINLOCH CASTLE
Isle of Rum
Invernessshire
Phone 0687 2037
An Edwardian country house frozen in time, Britain's least accessible and most eccentric hotel.

KNOCKINAAM
LODGE
Portpatrick
Wigtownshire
Phone 077681 471
Utterly charming hotel right on the sea. Simple, unpretentious, and very comfortable. Winner of 1992 Country House Hotel of the Year Award.

PITTODRIE HOUSE HOTEL
Pitcaple by Inverurie
Aberdeenshire
Phone (046 76) 444
An unpretentious country house hotel situated in the heart of Aberdeenshire castle country.

TIRORAN HOUSE HOTEL
Isle of Mull
Argyllshire
Phone 068 15 232
A comfortable former shooting lodge with very high standards of food and drink on one of the most beautiful western islands.

TULLICH LODGE
Ballater
Aberdeenshire
Phone 03397 55406
A Victorian country lodge set in beautiful surroundings in the heart of Deeside. Famous for its atmosphere and good food.

One of the most enjoyable ways to see the Highlands is from a train. The Royal Scotsman, a luxury hotel on wheels, takes you through some of the most spectacular country in Scotland.

Inquiries and reservations to: Abercrombie and Kent. Phone: U.S. (800) 323-3602; U.K. (071) 730 9600.

BIBLIOGRAPHY

The Best Fishing in Scotland by Lewis Ann Garner (Lochar, 1990).

Buildings of the Scottish Countryside by Robert J. Naismith (Gollancz, 1989).

Castles, Houses and Gardens of Scotland by Nan Patullo (Blackwood, 1967).

The Classical Country House in Scotland, 1660–1800 by James Macaulay (Faber and Faber, 1987).

A Concise History of Scotland by Fitzroy Maclean (Thames and Hudson, 1970).

Exploring Scotland's Heritage, series editor Anna Ritchie (Her Majesty's Stationery Office, 1985).

The Gardens of Queen Elizabeth The Queen Mother by The Marchioness of Salisbury (Viking, 1988).

The Highland Clans by Sir Iain Moncreiffe of that Ilk (Barrie and Jenkins, 1982).

Kinkell, The Reconstruction of a Scottish Castle by Gerald Laing (Ardullie House, 1984).

Rag Rugs by Emma Tennant (Walker Books, 1992).

Scottish Baronial Houses by Hubert Fenwick (Robert Hale, 1986).

Scottish Country Houses and Castles by Sheila Forman (George Outram, 1967).

Scottish Country Houses and Gardens by John Fleming (Country Life Limited, 1954).

Scottish Doocots by Tim Buxbaum (Shire Publications).

The Scottish Garden by Brinsley Burbidge and Fay Young (Moubray House Publishing, 1989).

Scottish Interiors, series editor Sheila Mackay (Moubray House Press, 1987).

Sir Walter Scott by David Daiches (Thames and Hudson, 1971).

The Story of Scotland in Stone by Ian C. Hannah (Oliver and Boyd, 1934).

Tartans by Christian Hesketh (Octopus Books, 1972).

Wildlife of Scotland, edited by Fred Holliday (Macmillan, 1979).

INDEX

239